BRIGHT NOTES

THE MAJOR PLAYS OF GEORGE BERNARD SHAW

Intelligent Education

Nashville, Tennessee

BRIGHT NOTES: The Major Plays of George Bernard Shaw
www.BrightNotes.com

ISBN: 978-1-645424-26-0 (Paperback)
ISBN: 978-1-645424-27-7 (eBook)

Published in accordance with the U.S. Copyright Office Orphan Works and Mass Digitization report of the register of copyrights, June 2015.

Originally published by Monarch Press.
Robert Rockman, 1964
2020 Edition published by Influence Publishers.

Interior design by Lapiz Digital Services. Cover Design by Thinkpen Designs.

Printed in the United States of America.

Library of Congress Cataloging-in-Publication Data forthcoming.
Names: Intelligent Education
Title: BRIGHT NOTES: The Major Plays of George Bernard Shaw
Subject: STU004000 STUDY AIDS / Book Notes

CONTENTS

PREFACE

The aims of this outline and commentary are several:

1. To present twelve plays of George Bernard Shaw in synopsis: six major plays in detailed summary and six less important plays in compressed summary.

2. To provide the reader with some description of Shaw's artistry: The method utilized is to apply a critical comment to the preface and *each act* of the major plays reviewed (to the whole play in the compressed summaries), followed by an analysis of some of the important characters in these plays. The intention is to show the reader what Shaw is like as a dramatist and to answer questions such as: How does Shaw construct a play? What techniques of dramatic craftsmanship does he favor? What problems of form do his plays present? What methods of characterization does he employ?

3. To show the developments in Shaw's thinking: In Bernard Shaw we find a primary example of what the critic Eric Bentley has called "The Playwright as Thinker." Shaw, as we shall see, is above all a dramatist of ideas. This study guide recognizes the obligation to help the reader in sorting out and placing Shaw's ideas in the

total philosophical scheme that the plays dramatize. Accordingly, the comments emphasize his ideas as ideas, sometimes divorcing them from their dramatic context for the sake of examination. In addition, this study guide presents the plays in the order of their composition so that one may see how Shaw's thinking (he thinks in and through his plays) and playwriting grew. Over the years Shaw was given to much repetition of idea and reiteration of theme, and the reader must expect a recurrence of familiar material. But it is useful to see Shaw in plays that range from *Arms and the Man* (1894) to *Saint Joan* (1923). These mark the limits of the period in which Shaw made his reputation. They provide the time limits of this guide; works composed outside this period are considered in the supplementary biographical and critical sections.

Two considerations are important: First, there is nothing inherently difficult about Shaw's language. His writing is often rich in allusion and reference, and wherever necessary this guide explains phrasing which may now be obscure. But Shaw's ideas are complex and at times the discussion presented here may seem overburdened with concepts, notably those on *Man and Superman* and of *Saint Joan,* where the issues dealt with are so large. To appreciate Shaw fully, it may be necessary for the reader to go back to the plays themselves and to their prefaces, where the connection of ideas and play will seem less artificial and more organic, less abstract and more immediate.

Second, this guide does not treat Shaw's non-dramatic works. The closest it comes to his purely expository writing is the summary of the prefaces to the major plays.

The critical comments cannot be exhaustive. They can only call attention to some ways of thinking about a play. They may invite the student to make further inquiry. Possibly he will find some of the review questions and answers helpful to his own thinking. Although these review questions and answers are grouped after the plays; the student may want to consult them as he goes through the outline play by play. Supplied at the close of the guide is a bibliography with suggestions for secondary reading.

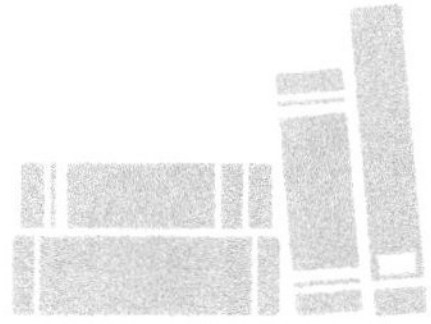

GEORGE BERNARD SHAW

INTRODUCTION TO GEORGE BERNARD SHAW

The life of George Bernard Shaw spanned nearly a century. It is important to note that he was born in 1856, before the American Civil War, and died in 1950, after the outbreak of the Korean War: a period which witnessed many important changes in civilization. In his years as a writer, Shaw was an active observer of these changes, especially of the emergence of the unsettling twentieth century out of the already complex nineteenth. Moreover, Shaw was a commentator on every aspect of the challenge the new century brought with it. Deeply committed to a description of this challenge, his interests were all-embracing, his mind encyclopedic, his energy unflagging. Altogether Shaw remains not only a significant modern dramatist but also one of the supreme all-round men of letters in English literature. Fashions vary and Shaw has been in and out of critical favor, but his place as one of the leading writers of our time is now secure.

HIS EARLY LIFE

He was born in Dublin, Ireland, on July 26, 1856, the youngest of three children and the only son of a shabby-genteel, incompatible couple. His formal schooling was irregular and a source of misery to him. He always said he learned more outside of school-from some of his uncles and from a friend of the family, a musician devoted to Mrs. Shaw who herself was a singer who encouraged her son to cultivate all the arts. Besides playing and hearing music at home. Shaw frequented the opera and the Dublin concert halls. He went often to the art galleries and the theatre and was a great reader of good literature. These pursuits helped to sustain him in the trying years of his youth, after the separation of his parents, and while he was working as an office boy to a land agent and living with his father.

LIFE IN LONDON

In 1876 Shaw joined his mother (now living and working in London) and tried earning his livelihood by writing. He wrote criticism intermittently, then five novels in succession. All of them were rejected by publishers; but, in 1884-1887, four of them appeared serially in literary magazines, attracting interest if not money. London was superior to Dublin as a center of intellectual and literary activity and Shaw devoted himself fully now to many new interests. He became a member of the newly formed British Fabian Socialist Society whose members were working for the gradual improvement of the harsh conditions under which the lower classes lived in industrial society. Shaw joined debating clubs, lectured on social questions, and read extensively at the British Museum Reading Room. In these years he managed to become a regular and eventually well-known reviewer of books, music, art, and drama.

FIRST PLAYS

In 1885 Shaw took the first step in his career of dramatist by writing a play about slum landlords. It did not reach the stage until 1892 and then it was produced by the new Independent Theatre Society, sponsors of untried and often controversial works for which a commercial production was out of the question. Three years before, the Society had given the first performance in England of Henrik Ibsen's *A Doll's House*, a major play by the idol-smashing Norwegian, and Shaw had written the first (and still important) book on Ibsen in our language, *The Quintessence of Ibsenism*. In it Shaw showed that Ibsen was introducing something new in the theatre and could be considered a revolutionary modern: he (Ibsen) was writing plays with a purpose, not just entertaining, time-killing confections.

Though his success was uncertain, Shaw became increasingly serious now about his own playwriting. By 1900 he wrote nine plays (and many non-dramatic pieces), four of which are treated below: *Arms and the Man*, *Candida*, *The Devil's Disciple*, and *Caesar and Cleopatra*. At first, these plays were generally more successful outside England, and only gradually did Shaw make an impression on the managers of London's commercial theatres. Undoubtedly all this activity took a toll on his health. In 1898 Shaw suffered a physical breakdown and decided to quit journalism and public speaking. Not that he abandoned interest in the cause of social reform. This he maintained in his dramatic and critical writing, notably in the prefaces of the published editions of his plays, for which he gained an audience not always given to theatre going. In the same year he married a well-to-do Irishwoman several years his senior, Charlotte Frances Payne-Townshend. She nursed him back to health, shared his interests, and spent her life from then on in providing Shaw with companionship and an atmosphere conducive to work.

THE MIDDLE PLAYS

1905 was an important year for Shaw-the success in London of his ambitious *Man and Superman* (written 1901-1903) and the beginning of the next phase of his advancing theatrical career. His earlier plays were now revived and studied for their meaning; his international reputation grew; and his new plays were welcomed. Ten of them followed between 1905 and the outbreak of World War I in 1914. Of interest here are *Major Barbara*, *Androcles and the Lion*, *Misalliance*, *Pygmalion*, and the play he began in 1913, *Heartbreak House*. During the war Shaw courted public disfavor by suggesting that warfare was questionable. But he continued to write, and in 1921 he brought out his longest play, one ripe in philosophical and **metaphysical** speculation: *Back to Methuselah*. In 1923 appeared the immensely successful historical play *Saint Joan* (discussed in this guide). In 1925 Shaw was awarded the Nobel Prize for Literature, the money from which he donated to a scheme for promoting the study of Scandinavian literature in English.

LATER LIFE

By this time Shaw was nearly seventy and a world figure, famous for his socialism, vegetarianism, his abstention from liquor and tobacco, his outspoken opinions and his eccentric dress. The plays that followed until 1940 were varied in their subject matter, uneven in their artistry, and yet astonishing coming from a man who might well have seen fit to retire. But Shaw chose to keep writing (even for the films) to make a world tour, to be interviewed on every conceivable question, to compile a collected edition of his works, and to write a book on politics in 1944. His last play was produced in 1947. His wife had died in 1943 and Shaw said he often felt lost without her. In 1950, in the garden at his remote Ayot St. Lawrence home, Shaw fell and after a siege of illness died on November 2. He wrote fifty-eight plays, of varying length. He wrote five novels and some short stories, at least two full-length books on politics and social organization, and several on art, literature, music. His numerous critical essays and journalistic writings have not yet been fully collected.

THE MAN

Because he was so prominent a figure for so many years, the public thought it knew Shaw well. To the superficial eye he seemed an intellectual entertainer given to the expression of often outrageous opinions redbearded and winking with glee at the shambles he made of the ordinary man's idea of the world and its institutions. To be sure, Shaw delighted in this reputation. In fact, he kept it alive, he admitted, to better accomplish the work he found necessary to his very existence. He lured the public into listening to him and made it laugh. Thereby he hoped to get it to pay him serious attention as a moral and social philosopher. This may seem something of a paradox, a kind of contradiction or apparent contradiction, and paradox is the key to the man and the plays. Appearing a jester, Shaw was fundamentally serious, idealistic, visionary, religious, and even mystical. He was a passionate man, too, but his passions were not ordinary ones. He seemed, for example, to have no place in his life for romantic love. Instead he devoted himself to the improvement of the world around him by the method he knew best, lecturing it in the theatre and on the page.

THE AIM IN THE THEATRE

Shaw considered himself an idealist with a mission. "Though my trade is that of a playwright," he wrote, "my vocation is that of a prophet." He would not write a line purely for idle entertainment, he warned, because it went against his soul to do so. He was not an enemy of entertainment or scornful of success. But he described himself as a Puritan reformer who used the drama as a weapon to oppose the worship by men of outworn creeds and conventions. As a Socialist, he was committed to a program for the betterment of society, and for that purpose he did not use the theatre alone. But Shaw found that the stage made an effective pulpit or platform and the theatre provided a ready-made audience. He did not mind being thought **didactic** or a crank as long as it was understood that he meant what he said. His comedy, he hoped, would be cleansing and his humor health-giving. As a man of the theatre, he was practical, shrewd, firm, businesslike, and unsentimental. In his life and his work Shaw was essentially a rationalist with much of the poet in him. As he has one of his characters put it, he wanted "Life with a blessing," and he dedicated himself to showing that it can be achieved by scrupulous self-criticism and by close examination of the world around oneself. Shaw was not a naive optimist or, though he had his dark moods, an unthinking pessimist. He believed that one has to work for one's dreams, and the better the dream, the better the man. His religion was that of the Life Force (see below, *Man and Superman*), the surrendering oneself to the hard will of the universe that compels one to strive, to fret away one's petty complaints, and to keep striving.

THE TEMPER OF THE PLAYS

All this might lead one to think that the plays are formidable, but they are not. They are, largely speaking, serious comedies of modern life that make a discussion of issues relevant to living in the twentieth century. Not that they are glumly or clinically analytical. They are philosophical in their reach, witty and ironic in temper, and their thematic interest and comic energy derive from the interplay of characters and ideas. Shaw frequently enjoys identifying a character with a particular idea and then exploding this idea from under him by showing up its inadequacy as a guide to life or its falseness as an item of belief. Thus, in the first play of the outline, *Arms and the Man*, Sergius is made to see that his notions of love and war have made a fool of him and that Bluntschli, in his more realistic appraisal of things, living without illusions is the man who suffers less. When Shaw approves of an idea or set of ideas, he usually makes his hero or heroine the exponent of it. The contest in his major plays is between a hero of dynamic vision or insight and the characters or system that oppose all he stands for. In the conflict that is the substance of the play, the hero must win over or defeat his antagonists by irrefutable logic, sheer wit, or courageous commitment to a course of action. Dick Dudgeon (*The Devil's Disciple*) puts down his adversaries by a combination of daring and unconventionality; Caesar (*Caesar and Cleopatra*) is a superior being because he is an idealist with ideals that he can show to be practical and workable. But the opposing system can win and the hero a philosophic man or genius, be defeated. In *Saint Joan*, one of Shaw's several history plays and his only tragedy, the heroine is tragically overcome because the world is not ready for her. Sometimes the defeat is not so drastic, as in *Man and Superman*, where the man of moral passion, Tanner, is brought willingly to heel by the woman who pursues him. We may have, then, depending upon the victory or defeat of the hero, pure comedy, pure tragedy, or tragicomedy.

FORM OF THE PLAYS

It is not always easy to pigeonhole a Shaw play in an accepted category of drama. At the outset of his playwriting career Shaw constructed his drama on the model of the neatly structured French "well made play." But by 1900 he was already looking for a freer form and before long Shaw virtually invented a new form, the drama of discussion or ideas with comic, tragic, or farcical overtones, mixing all three when he saw the occasion. Shaw's originality lies in his taking the discussion play of life, (modern or otherwise), in its purest form, as made popular by Ibsen and some English adaptors, and infusing in it the spirit of English comedy as practiced from the seventeenth century to his own day. In many of Shaw's plays, one feels the presence of earlier English comic writers like the Elizabethan Ben Jonson, Goldsmith and Sheridan of the eighteenth century, or the novelist Dickens of the nineteenth. Shaw is specific enough in alerting us to his models. He ranges far afield, beyond England, in fact, invoking the satiric spirit of Aristophanes or Moliere. But if we read Shaw carelessly, his insistence upon the logic, consistency, and reality or his situations, characters, and **themes** may divert us from seeing that in their techniques, his plays are anything but "realistic" imitations of life. Despite their discussion of social or moral dilemmas, they are not as earthbound as these terms might apply. They are never, for example, documentary or minutely psychological. The characters are recognizable enough in speech or behavior. Shaw accurately struck off a number of contemporary types; but he has an overriding concern for them not as "lifelike" characters, but as representatives of a point of view, a debatable idea, a moral posture. It is safe to say that in great measure, Shaw's dramatic methods are akin to those of artificial comedy. In the major comedies, for all their seriousness as criticisms of ideas or institutions, Shaw is closer to Oscar Wilde's *The Importance of Being Earnest* than he is to

Ibsen's *Ghosts*. The requisites of this kind of play are energy, invention, speed, surprise, brilliance of dialogue, larger-than-life characterization, and exaggeration - all of which abound in Shaw's plays. They are assured in their language too. The characters usually speak like the literate person of Shaw's day, unless Shaw is depicting the accent or dialect of a particular class. Shaw never tries to portray the faltering hesitation of slackness that passes for the idiom of "realistic" speech in much contemporary drama. He is never photographic, nor does he have the ear of a tape recorder. The rhythms of a characteristic Shavian speech are firm, emphatic, controlled, and expressive of a particular cast of mind or social attitude. His speeches may seem highly constructed, unspontaneous, deliberate, and to some, old-fashioned. They are close in style to the writing in the prefaces, where we hear the distinctive voice of Shaw the essayist, the author of some of the most forceful, powerful prose of this century.

SOME FAULTS OF THE PLAYS

The plays have faults. They are usually well constructed but occasionally arbitrary in invention or resolution. When we feel something mechanical or unconvincing at work, it is frequently because Shaw has gone too far in enjoying himself. It is possible that we may feel that ideas are being too cleverly manipulated. The typical Shaw play makes its points and often its climaxes by taking an accepted, received, or common idea and inverting it, standing it on its head, so to speak, or playing a variation on it. This serves to surprise, delight, or outrage us by the unfamiliar turn given to the familiar. In *Man and Superman*, Ann Whitefield is at first seen to be a modest, properly Victorian young woman; nobody will believe John Tanner when he says she is the opposite to what she seems. In time she is shown pursuing him, not waiting to be pursued, and the play's position is that this is what a woman by nature must be: not to languish and wait to be wooed but rather to go after her man. But in *Pygmalion* we are asked to believe that Alfred Doolittle, a trash collector who amuses Professor Higgins by his skill in outwitting middle-class mores, can be regarded by other as the prophet of a new morality. Even for a play that never attempts to be literal in its probability, that has elements of a myth or fairy tale, the joke may seem a little too good. Sometimes we may balk at Shaw's prankishness, however sympathetic we are to the main intentions of his play. In *Caesar and Cleopatra*, is the scene of Caesar's throwing Cleopatra into the harbor at Alexandria and then leaping in himself very attractive? It is spectacular and serves Shaw's purpose of deglamorizing those nearly mythical characters, but it may leave one uneasy by its whimsicality.

CHARACTER AND IDEA

In making his plays depend so heavily on the working out of what he might call an ideological position, in making discussion and debate so central in his plays, Shaw takes artistic risks. Were he not so often skillful at coordinating character and idea, and thereby allowing us to feel the human weight of a supporting personality and circumstance behind the idea, he might well sink his plays. As it is, some critics find Shaw's plays abstract; all ideas and not enough believable character. One can only say in refutation that we should consider Shaw at his best. Take scene four of *Saint Joan*. The men assembled in Warwick's tent hold all the issues of the play in hand, and the stand that each one takes intellectually and morally is the stuff of this scene. Shaw keeps their deliberations dramatically alive by showing us how much of each man's character is bound up with the ideas he advances. Warwick's very existence depends upon his crushing out Joan's rebelliousness and all that it stands for in the way of new political alignments; Cauchon must defend himself and the Church from her Protestantism; and poor de Stogumber is naively committed to a defense of his country right or wrong - and so to the destruction of the Maid. This scene does not become static-though there is not much superficial stage action because the characters are seated. It may be argued that in this instance Shaw makes the play humanly interesting not despite the presence of ideas but actually because of them.

CRITICISM OF SHAW'S PLAYS

Critics of Shaw have been divided on this matter from the start, and it provides perhaps the major issue in assessments of the playwright, one whereby the varying fortunes of his reputation may be traced. Louis Kronenberger, a present-day critic, has called Shaw a "showman of ideas," but there have been many who accuse Shaw of crudely making of his characters mouthpieces for his ideas and so denying them independent life. Perhaps dramatic criticism is in need of repair here, because the whole notion of how much life a character need have is open to question. One must repeat that Shaw's plays are not to be judged by the standards we bring to an evaluation of a faithfully representational drama of contemporary life. Long ago the Irish poet W. B. Yeats reported a dream he had of a sewing machine that looked like Shaw and that clacked on and on and would not stop. He was making a point about Shaw's unrelenting examination of modern life, the tone and style of which Yeats found offensive. In some of Shaw's very late plays, one does hear Shaw "clacking on and on." Characters go undifferentiated, we feel that they are only walking ideas and not very sound ideas at that. This rarely happens in the major plays, however.

At their best, one can distinguish in them the voices one hears, as Professor Reuben Brower has pointed out in the instance of *Man and Superman* (see his commentary on Shaw and analysis of the play in the second volume of *Major British Writers*, G. B. Harrison (Ed.), 1954). Then we view each character as a separate dramatic force, as we are meant to, and the obstacle allegedly put there by the presence of ideas in a play seems to disappear.

In short, one must not be misled by the attention of so much Shaw criticism to ideas. Too much of it has been taken up with evaluations of his philosophy or with attempts to prove that the plays are outmoded because of their content. Later generations have not always been able to find any urgency in Shaw's religion of the Life Force. Perhaps, more legitimately they protest his device of inverting ideas. But Shaw should not be disregarded as a journalist or pamphleteer. Even as such he is a superior writer, with a style that commands respect by its vigor, forcefulness, and conviction.

RECENT CRITICISM AND SCHOLARSHIP

Fortunately, the easy dismissal of Shaw as a major playwright is coming to an end. In the 1930s, the poet T. S. Eliot, in the name of pure literature, could find no place for Shaw or ideas. But even before Shaw's death, critics were paying him new respect. Thus, Eric Bentley's *Bernard Shaw* (1947) tries to clear away confusions about Shaw as a playwright and view him as an artist. Lately, scholars have been inquiring into Shaw's intellectual background (Julian B. Kaye, *Bernard Shaw and the Nineteenth-Century Tradition*, 1958), examining his **themes** and characters (A. H. Nethercot, *Men and Supermen: The Shavian Portrait Gallery*, 1954), and finding, it would seem, more than ever to say about his dramatic and theatrical practice (the Shaw issue of

Modern Drama 2, September, 1959). In the theatre, Shaw's place is secure. The revivals of his plays go on undiminished in number. Since World War II her seems to be finding a new generation for audience. And the publication of more of his non-dramatic pieces continues. We are promised soon a complete edition of his letters. It is not necessary to accept Shaw's greatness without qualification. But to deny him significance is to reject a part of the twentieth century. He is an education in himself. Writing of Shaw's plays, the American critic Edmund Wilson has said that we may find in them a developing "chronicle of a soul in relation to society." If we were to read Shaw for that alone, it would be reason enough.

GEORGE BERNARD SHAW

ARMS AND THE MAN

HISTORICAL BACKGROUND

The setting is a small town in Bulgaria in November, 1885. This was a troubled time for the Balkan states, threatened by the Turks and divided among themselves. While the Turks were preparing to invade, one of the states, Serbia, suddenly declared war on another, Bulgaria, which caused the Russians, allies of Bulgaria, to withdraw military support from that country. Left alone, poorly trained and equipped, the Bulgarian army surprised everyone by winning a signal victory at the village of Slivnitza in Bulgaria, another a few days later, and then by crossing the frontier into Serbia itself. At this point Austria, fearing a general outbreak of war and disruption of her Empire, intervened to negotiate a peace by the Treaty of Bucharest in March, 1886. All of these circumstances are referred to directly or indirectly in the course of the play. As for the title, it is derived from the opening lines of Virgil's ancient Latin poem *The Aeneid*: "Arms and the man I sing. . . ."

CHARACTERS

Bluntschli

A Swiss, about thirty-five, serving as a professional soldier, an officer, in the Serbian army.

Raina

The heroine, a romantic Bulgarian girl of twenty-three.

Sergius

A handsome, moody young officer, Raina's friend and hero.

Major Petkoff

Raina's father.

Catherine

Raina's mother.

Louka

A woman servant in the Petkoff household, young, attractive.

Nicola

A middle-aged man servant.

Russian Officer

in Bulgarian uniform (Act I).

PREFACE

Preface (to the volume of *Plays Pleasant*, 1898). Shaw does not tell us very much about this play or even about the other plays included in the volume which this preface heads. He primarily reviews his career as a writer of "New Drama," a term that describes the plays considered advanced and even experimental in their day, produced for small audiences and not considered as having appeal for large popular theatres. Ibsen was part of the new movement or directions in drama, the Irish poet W. B. Yeats, and in great measure Shaw himself. Shaw advances and defends his conception of a theatre and drama devoted to a purpose greater than commercial entertainment for the unthinking, easily satisfied playgoers. To him the theatre is an important institution in the life of a nation, as important as the church or the law, whereby men become intellectually conscious of the lives they lead and the civilization they make. They must not be pandered to with fictitious inventions and seductive lies about the nature of reality. The theatre should be subsidized or supported by the state, and theatrical managers relieved of coping with the risky finances of theatrical production. In short, the theatre can be a place for (1) instruction in the true character of social institutions, (2) a platform for the dramatized analysis of genuine versus false idealism, and (3) an instrument to expose sham romantic conventions.

Comment

This preface is important in its statements about the theatre and the New Drama. Its interest is autobiographical and philosophical. Shaw outlines some of the steps he has taken in his career to this date and sets down the fundamentals of his dramatic and theatrical credo. Much of what he has to say in later prefaces and in some of the later plays has a beginning here.

ACT ONE

Setting

Raina's bedroom. A night in November, 1885. Catherine Petkoff hastily enters her daughter Raina's bedroom and excitedly reports the Bulgarian victory at the battle of Slivnitza (see above, Introduction). She is especially excited by the news that Raina's fiance Sergius is said to the hero of the hour, having acted without orders and led a splendid charge that scattered the Serbo-Austrian enemy. Raina is happy to hear this, for it reassures her, as she tells her mother, that the heroic ideals she cherishes are real and not imaginary, vital and not just learned from books and plays, that Sergius' bravery, which she had secretly doubted, is now proved genuine. The servant girl Louka comes in at this point, with information that Serbian fugitives are being chased and may have run into town; there may be shooting, and she urges her mistress to close the windows and make fast the shutters. Catherine goes to check the house, and Louka, after showing Raina how to open and close the shutters, goes out too. Raina, alone, takes up a portrait of Sergius, addresses words of reverence to it, then prepares to read herself to sleep. Shots break the night-time quiet, coming closer. Raina scrambles from bed to blow out her candle, then hurries back. Suddenly there is the sound of the shutters being opened from outside, and a figure drops into the room and scratches a match to get some light.

Crouching on the bed, Raina sees a young man (Bluntschli) in the torn, mud-and-blood spattered uniform of a Serbian artillery officer. He warns her to be quiet, informs her he is being pursued and has no hesitation in shooting her or anyone else. With a quick intuition that he is dealing with a young woman of means and social pretension, he keeps her cloak from Raina, in the thought that she will be too modest to let anyone into her room in her nightdress. A disturbance is heard in the house as a search party enters almost forcibly. Then Louka is knocking at Raina's door. The fugitive changes his mind and kindly returns Raina's cloak, deciding to make a stand with his sabre. But, on an impulse, Raina says she can save him and gets him to hide behind the curtains. Her mother, Louka, and a Russian officer (in Bulgarian uniform) come in to inspect the balcony up which an escaped soldier has been seen climbing. Raina denies having seen anyone, and with apologies the officer leaves. But Louka has seen something, the revolver the fugitive has thrown down on the ottoman, and with an insolent laugh she goes out.

Raina locks the door and turns to the man she has saved. He identifies himself as a Swiss and a professional soldier who fights for pay, then asks if he might stay a few minutes to collect himself. Raina sits on his pistol, which causes her to jump up with a scream. He tells her it is not loaded, that he has no ammunition and always carries chocolate instead of cartridges, which surprises her and offends her ideals of manhood. But she offers him sweets from a box, while he tells her that only the inexperienced soldiers carry ammunition, the veterans always food. He goes on to commend the success of the Bulgarian victory but describes the cavalry charge against the Serbs as unprofessional. Raina thinks the leader of it a hero, the man he describes as melodramatic, foolhardy, operatic soldier who risked his troops unnecessarily and won out of sheer luck. She gets up and takes the portrait of Sergius and presents it to this stranger, who confirms that the original was the man he has been describing. Angry now, Raina orders the fugitive to leave, his punishment for suggesting her lover is less than a hero. But the man is worn out and tells her she may give the alarm if she wants to. She is overcome by pity now but does not know where she can keep him hidden. Seeing the justice of this, he rises sleepily and is about to climb down the balcony to the street when she pulls him back at the sound of renewed gunfire. She tells him that she is the daughter of the well-to-do Major Petkoff, whose hospitality he may trust in this house which she proudly describes as having an inside staircase and the only library in Bulgaria. She compares his refuge to that given a character in an opera she has seen in Bucharest, where the hospitality of a nobleman was sacred and inviolable. He tells her in turn that his father owns six hotels in Switzerland, and kisses her hand. Raina is on the point of fetching her mother when she sees him falling asleep. He promises not to doze, but when she has left the room he collapses in fatigue on the ottoman. Raina returns with Catherine, who tries to shake the stranger awake, but Raina stops her with "the poor darling is worn out. Let him sleep." Which causes her mother to turn in surprise and look sternly at Raina.

Comment

One should always begin a Shaw play by attending carefully to the stage directions. In their fullness they are much like the descriptions of place and character one finds in many novels. Notice, for example, the statement about the decoration of Raina's room being "not like anything to be seen in the west of Europe. It is half rich-Bulgarian, half cheap-Viennese." At once we can place the Petkoffs socially and culturally. They are rich, in a heavily Bulgarian, that is, semi-Eastern, semi-primitive way and have aspirations to the sophistication represented by the more Western-oriented Vienna. Keeping this in mind, we understand the significance of Raina's informing the escaping Bluntschli that her house contains an inside staircase and a library and that she goes to the opera in Bucharest. She wants this Swiss soldier to think her fully cultivated and not provincial. (Besides, it is in the opera house and in literature that she finds her models of heroism.) This affectation is comic. Note, too, the description of Catherine: "Determined to be a Viennese lady." Mother and daughter are alike in ideas and ideals. The details, then, about environment and about character are meaningful in an appreciation of the total dramatic action. In this play affectation, romance, and misguided idealism will all be challenged. Also, this first act is interesting for the way it establishes one **theme** of the play: Bluntschli's (hear the word "blunt" in the Swiss name) realistic view of soldiering versus Raina's love of storybook heroics. The chocolate soldier (an operetta based on *Arms and the Man* was made by Oscar Straus under that title) affronts Raina by his depreciation of Sergius' headlong cavalry charge. For him it is false and melodramatic. And this view is put forward in a play that begins as melodramatically as any could, with a fugitive hiding in a young lady's bedroom, where he may be trapped and forced to fight for his life. This arrangement of events is deliberate, of course, and may well be considered ironic, as though Shaw were mocking himself as well as the run-of-the-mill stage melodramas that were common on the late nineteenth century stage.

ACT TWO

Setting

The garden of the Petkoff house. A morning in March, 1886, several days after the peace.

Nicola, a cautious, middle-aged servant, is warning Louka to mend her ways and not be disrespectful to any of the Petkoffs. If she quarrels with them, he will not marry her because he is dependent on their good will. She must, he says, be discreet, keep whatever she knows about Raina or anyone in the house to herself, or she will be ruined as a servant and her relations will feel the consequences too. Louka pertly replies that Nicola has the soul of a servant. They hear someone calling, and in a moment Major Petkoff, back from the war, enters, as Louka goes into the house for fresh coffee. Catherine comes in and welcomes her husband affectionately. They discuss the peace treaty and his health, and the importance of having impressed the Russian officers attached to the Bulgarian army with the cultivation of the Petkoff household.

Now Major Sergius Saranoff arrives, a handsome young man with an air of great sensitivity and moodiness. Petkoff and Catherine greet him warmly, and Catherine congratulates him on his now famous charge against the Serbs. But he replies to his prospective mother-in-law that he has made too many commanders uncomfortable by his daring and originality and that his army career is over (shortly before, Petkoff told Catherine

Sergius would never be promoted). He is going to submit his resignation. Catherine is shocked and wants this model hero to withdraw such a request. Raina very prettily comes in at this moment and Sergius chivalrously drops to one knee to kiss her hand. She welcomes her father home, and they take up again the subject of Sergius' military career. Sergius complains that soldiering is too much of a trade or business proposition these days and not for him. Witness, he says, the shrewd dealing of that Swiss officer, a volunteer in the Serbian army, who made such a clever bargain during the exchange of prisoners, getting the Bulgarians to trade able-bodied men for worn out horses. Petkoff encourages Sergius to repeat the story another officer has told them about the Swiss's rescue after the charge by two Bulgarian ladies. The women hear this, recognizing, of course, how they have been betrayed; Raina is offended by the story, though she does not reveal the true reason for her displeasure. Sergius apologizes, however, and is about to follow Petkoff on some army business, when Catherine draws her husband away and leaves the young couple together.

Raina addresses Sergius as her "hero" and her "king," and in return he compares his exploits in battle to those done by a knight of old at a tournament with his lady looking on. Raina believes theirs must be a higher love. She goes to get her hat so that they may go walking and leaves him in the garden, inspired by the nobleness and beauty of his feelings. He is alone but a moment. Louka comes in with coffee and he swaggers over to her to ask if she knows what the higher love is. He is very dashing now and quite pleased with himself. Suddenly he seizes the girl, then slips his hand around her waist. She begs him to be careful not to be seen, but he is reckless in this new mood of bravado and abandonment and tries to kiss her. She reproaches him and confesses she will never understand gentlefolk, his making love to her behind Raina's back and Raina's doing the same behind his. Sergius tries to check her accusations about Raina, but the information stings him as Louka intends it should. He strikes his forehead theatrically, tormented by the question of what kind of man he really is, so many men seem to exist in him-a hero, a clown, a fraud, a deceiver. Still, he must know who his rival is, but Louka will not tell him. Soon she admits she never saw but only heard the voice of the man in Raina's room, but she knows that if he ever came back, he is the one Miss Raina will marry whether the gentleman likes it or not. Sergius angrily grips Louka, then releases her, accusing her of being common and a servant. She retaliates by calling him a liar and claiming she is worth six or Raina. When she starts to leave, Sergius stops her, wanting to apologize for having hurt a woman. She does not want money from him but a kiss on her bruised arm. This he will not give, and with dignity she takes up the coffee things to return to the house, passing Raina on her way back to the garden. Catherine comes back too, and asks Sergius to go up the house a moment and help her confused husband with his military problems.

Catherine and Raina are angry with Bluntschli for having told on them, and Catherine notes that Petkoff has already asked for an old brown coat they sent Bluntschli off in that night. She observes too that Sergius will certainly break their engagement if he learns the truth. But now Raina says she does not care, that she has always felt a longing to shock the too-perfect Sergius, to scandalized him, after which she walks off and out of sight. At this point Louka returns to announce that a Serbian officer wishes to see the madam, and she hands Catherine a ticket signed "Captain Blunschli." Louka thinks he is Swiss and says he is carrying a large carpetbag. Catherine realizes it is Raina's intruder and that he has come to return the coat, and at such an unlucky moment, with Saranoff and her husband in the house! But it is too late for precautions. Suddenly Blunschli walks down the steps leading to the garden. Catherine goes to Bluntschli and hastily explains the situation, urging him to leave to once without saying anything. He agrees, says he wants only to leave the coat with a servant and go. He pauses to write out the address where his bag may be sent to him, but the delay is long enough to bring Petkoff and Sergius back from the house. At once Petkoff recognizes the officer who made the horse trade with him and Sergius and asks Bluntschli's help in solving the new problem he is having about the disposal of cavalry regiments. They are about to go back to the house, as Raina returns and cries out, "Oh! The chocolate-cream soldier!" All are amazed, and she explains that she was thinking of a chocolate pudding Louka spoiled that morning by setting plates on it. But Bluntschli understands. Nicola comes in with the carpetbag, but Catherine denies having asked him to bring the Captain's luggage into the garden. When Petkoff angrily criticizes Louka's stupidity about ruining Raina's pudding, the poor man does not know what is happening, and losing control, drops the bag on Petkoff's foot. The women calm Petkoff and he asks Bluntschli to stay with them a while before returning to Switzerland. Sergius presses him to stay, and Raina, (but not Catherine, who wants him to go), and Bluntschli, smiling, submits to their wishes.

Comment

This second act is taken up with complicating the plot, with arranging the events of the drama in an intricately comic way. Note how much the action depends upon comic deceptions or self-deceptions: (1) Catherine and Raina have their secret, the chocolate-cream soldier, and Raina, to avoid giving herself away, must pretend, when Sergius tells his story, that she is shocked by the coarseness of it; (2) Sergius is in a sense deceiving Raina when he lets her believe that theirs is a higher love and then tries to make love to her maid. Of course, he does not understand himself and admits he is a deceiver. And Raina is deceiving herself and him by talking of their exalted love at the same time she feels the urge to shock him; (3) when she sees the chocolate soldier, Raina accounts for her surprise by inventing the excuse about the pudding. There is a great deal of enjoyment for the audience in seeing the confusion caused by these deceptions. Note how poor Nicola is made the butt of them and loses his self-possession in the last minutes of the act. Contrast this with the opening pages, where the perfect servant gives realistic advice to the rebellious Louka. The methods of this act are often those of farce, a form of play in which misunderstanding, deception and counterdeception, and broad physical comedy are allowed to run riot. Not that *Arms and the Man* is, technically, a farce; it is more a comedy of character and of opposed points of view.

ACT THREE

Setting

The library, after lunch. The scene is in the library the Petkoffs spoke so well of but that we can see is ordinary. Bluntschli is at a kitchen table which serves as a desk; Sergius watches him, envious of the Captain's efficiency but scorning the nature of the work itself; Petkoff is smoking his waterpipe; Catherine is embroidering; Raina is daydreaming over a novel. The Major, comfortably fed and relaxed, asks after his old brown coat and does not believe his wife can find it, as she says she can when she rings for Nicola and sends him to fetch it from the blue closet. In a spirit of challenge, bets are taken all around in favor of Nicola's finding it, and the major is astonished when Nicola comes in with the coat. Now the military business is finished and all leave the room but Bluntschli and Raina. Raina tells the Swiss how his story about hiding in her room was repeated to Sergius and her father, and she assures him Sergius would challenge him to a duel if he knew. She has lied twice for Bluntschli's sake but does not, she tells him, want to be thought a lying woman by nature. But Bluntschli seems skeptical. He admires, he says, the noble attitude she strikes and the thrilling voice in which she declares herself truthful, but when she uses them on him he finds it impossible to believe a word she says. At first she is outraged, then gives in completely, saying he has found her out, that he is the first man who did not take her seriously. Oh no, he has! Corrects Bluntschli, but in his way, not hers. She confesses she has fooled her parents for years and Sergius, who, she admits, is himself fond of striking attitudes and gestures. She is happy to see that Bluntschli does not despise her for it and asks about the portrait of herself she gave him, which she put in an inside pocket of the brown coat the night of his escape. He has never found it, it must be there still, says Bluntschli. Raina is distressed to hear this because she has written something on it that she will not be able to justify to her father should he discover the portrait. Louka enters with mail and telegrams for Bluntschli, among which is a message that his father has died in Switzerland. He must leave in an hour, and so he goes out to give orders for preparations. Stung by his negligence in the business of the portrait, Raina comments to Louka on the Captain's lack of heart in failing to express grief for his loss, and angrily ascribes such a lack to all soldiers.

As she leaves, Nicola comes in with wood for the stove and eager to have a few words with Louka. She has been spurning his attention lately and is still not very compliant, even when he shows her the tips Sergius and Bluntschli have given him, all of which will go into saving for the shop he wants to open. He wants better treatment from Louka and reminds her, for all her contempt of him, that it is he who has trained her and taught her to be a woman instead of a coarse peasant girl. He gives her some good advice on how to behave like a lady instead of an upstart, and she admits that when he speaks in such coldblooded wisdom he takes all the rebelliousness and courage out of her. They are interrupted by the entrance of Sergius, but Nicola makes an excuse and leaves the officer with Louka. Sergius takes up with her where they left off in Act II. He assures her he is not trifling with her nor is he sorry about the bruise he gave her. He is a brave man, he says, his courage real, as he found in battle. But Louka accuses him of having only a schoolboy's courage, not the kind of courage, for example, that would make him love her in disregard of all social barriers between servant and master, as she would love him were she in a superior position. He assures her he would indeed love her bravely if he were not already in love with a better woman, Raina. And Louka shocks him by saying Raina will marry only Bluntschli, after which she, Louka, will have the pleasure of rejecting the craven Sergius. He is furious and seizes her fiercely. But again he gives way to despair, doubting himself, then tells Louka she belongs to him and if he chooses to love her he will marry her. She dares him to keep his word and says she will not wait long.

Bluntschli, unconcerned and looking over some papers, enters the library, and is surprised to hear Sergius address him as a rival and offer to meet him in a duel. But he accepts the challenge coolly and rationally, which angers Sergius, who is now playing the romantic hothead. Raina comes in and hears their conversation. Sergius then accuses her of loving Bluntschli and Bluntschli of having received her favors in her room in the middle of the night. He misunderstands what Louka tauntingly told him and does not realize that Bluntschli was hiding there to escape the Serbs, and when he is now put straight he is completely taken aback. War comes to seem a fraud to him and love as well. Now it is Raina's turn to be disillusioned, as she realizes Sergius has been making love to Louka, which she herself saw from her window. Sergius changes his mind, calls off the duel, alleging that Bluntschli is not a person to fight with - he has no romance about him, he is too reasonable, too much of a machine. Raina chooses to be sarcastic at this moment, as she urges Sergius, if he must have a rival, to fight Nicola, who after all is engaged to Louka. Then she angrily turns her back on him, after accusing him of employing Louka to spy on her and Bluntschli. The Swiss Captain now tries to settle their quarrel. He decides to send for Louka, who, Raina says, is probably listening at the door, and Sergius goes out and brings her back. Louka admits she has been eavesdropping, her love being at stake.

At this moment Petkoff enters, complaining that his coat is all out of shape because someone has been wearing it, then sends Louka to get it from Catherine. But Nicola arrives with it, Raina helps her father into it, and as she does so, very deftly removes from the inside pocket the photograph inscribed "Raina, to Her Chocolate-Cream Soldier." Bluntschli covers it with a piece of paper, while Sergius looks on with intense suspiciousness. Petkoff, talking on about it, is amazed to find the photograph gone, and asks if Sergius is not the chocolate-cream soldier. Sergius replies he is not. Bluntschli confesses he is and discloses that he was the fugitive that November night. Petkoff wants some clarification of things from Raina. She is not, she says firmly, engaged to either Sergius or Bluntschli, and Louka is the object of Sergius' affections. Petkoff is even more confused by Nicola's report that he is not engaged to Louka because she has a soul above her station, though he hopes for her custom at his shop should she marry into the nobility. Now Louka claims to have been insulted by everyone present and demands apology. Sergius, in a grand manner, on bended knee, apologizes, and she forgives him, accepting him as a husband. Bluntschli approves these heroics of Sergius, commenting that they have their practical side. But to Catherine, coming in now and finding

Louka in Sergius' arms, these heroics are an affront for which she wants an explanation. Things move quickly, though Bluntschli tries to minimize Raina's affection for him. How can she love him, a coarse Swiss soldier, a vagabond with a romantic disposition? Sergius cuts in to ask about that last surprising phrase. Yes, says Bluntschli, he is incurably romantic and has always been. Witness his night's adventure, not the most practical way to escape the enemy, or coming back as he has, just to get another look at Raina. And as for her, how can their affair be serious? Consider the photograph and the inscription. All of this happens too quickly for Petkoff, who is astonished to learn about the coat and the missing picture. But Raina is offended to be thought a silly schoolgirl when she is a woman of twenty-three, and she tears up the photograph and throws the pieces at Bluntschli. Sergius is really disillusioned now: War, love, and Bluntschi's practicality have all proved a fraud. Bluntschli considers quickly. He is not too old for Raina as he had thought, and he formally asks Petkoff for her hand. Catherine interposes with a reminder that the Petkoffs are an historically important family: They go back twenty years. And, as the Major reminds him, Raina is used to certain comforts. That proves no obstacle. Bluntschli reads from the papers he has received in the mail from Switzerland. At the hotels he has inherited from his father he has hundreds of horses, dozens of carriages, thousands of blankets and other household goods, besides possessing medals for distinguished service and claiming the standing of an officer and a gentleman; and he is a free citizen of Switzerland. All of this is good enough for Petkoff and Catherine, but Raina withholds her consent to a marriage, until Bluntschli catches her by the shoulders and wheels her about to face him as she did the chocolate-cream soldier. At this reminder of their first meeting, she softens and smiles shyly. Bluntschli is delighted and then immediately businesslike. In a quick change from romance to practical affairs, he gives Sergius instructions for disposing of the Serbian troops, then makes them all a brisk military bow and leaves for Switzerland, promising to be back soon. It is an admiring Sergius who exclaims: "What a man!" and then asks, "Is he a man?"

Comment

The best part of the comedy in this last act consists of the revelations of fundamental character and the settlement of conflicts. Raina is the first to be exposed, as she admits to Bluntschli that she always been something of a play-actress with her family and with Sergius. The Swiss is charmed by her and infatuated, but is not fooled. His way with her is direct. Note in the last scene how he takes her by the shoulders and makes her confront him squarely; he tolerates no coyness, no striking of attitudes. The disclosure that he is a romantic at heart is another surprise. We have been so used to seeing him as cool-headed and unperturbed (note the calm way he accepts Sergius' challenge) that we are not prepared to hear him admit to an incurably romantic disposition. No wonder Sergius is in a muddle. He is supposed to be the romantic of this play, the man unsettled by the realization that war and love are filled with empty posturings; when he learns that even the practical man is not wise he is all the more cynical. He and Raina have been playing a game of hero worship, but his nature gets the better of him and he makes love to Louka, she by working on his love of the romantically difficult (a marriage between a servant and a man of the upper classes), wins him. It is a relief for him to come down to a more earthly love after the over-idealized and abstract worship of Raina. It is by these revelations and discoveries that complications are resolved and the way made for the happy ending of the play. There is comedy as well in the confusion of poor Petkoff, distracted and unintentionally made sport of by the other characters.

ANALYSIS OF SELECTED CHARACTERS

Raina

She is well-bred in a provincial way, and her reading and opera-going have gone to her head. She takes the life she finds there as a model for reality and expects men and women to live up to literary patterns of melodramatic heroism and love-making. A genuine woman of spirit and sense is somewhat obscured by her devotion to these models, and it takes Bluntschli to find her. By his rationality and unexcitable disposition to see things as they are, he cuts through her pretentions and gets part her guard. He is very impressive to her, even as she is provoked by his bluntness, and after his daredevil entry to her room there is really no other man for her, as Louka so rightly insists.

Bluntschli

A man of thirty-five, he is clearsighted and wise about the world. As a professional soldier, he knows that the veterans save their lives by following, not leading a charge; that war is hell and not (as Sergius and Raina think) an arena for the foolhardy display of heroics; that chocolate is more important in sustaining a soldier than a beltful of cartridges. Sergius thinks that Bluntschli is only a commercial-minded hotelkeeper at heart and has no poetry in him. But he has, and he surprises everyone by owning up to a romantic character underneath his appearance of complete soberness.

Sergius

He is referred to in the stage directions as Byronic in temperament. Shaw means that he is given to the fashionable melancholy and moodiness made popular by the characters of Byron's poems (and by Byron himself) in early nineteenth-century England. Byron's heroes search for the ideal, the intangible and unattainable, are disillusioned by finding that life does not live up to their expectations, and sometimes turn cynical. In Sergius some of these traits are exaggerated to the point of making him seem a comic posturer, but his despair at not knowing what kind of man he is meant to be genuine.

Louka

An independent young woman who combines romance and practicality in her nature. She dares to rise above her station, to the dismay of Nicola, and brings off a storybook triumph - the wedding of the maid servant to her master. Sergius finds that her directness, even her laughing at him, brings him into a welcome contract with reality that neither his own nature nor Raina's hero worship provides.

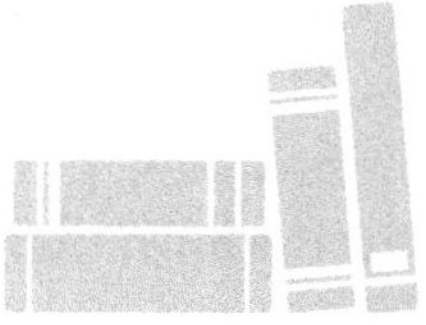

GEORGE BERNARD SHAW

CAESAR AND CLEOPATRA

INTRODUCTION

By "history" Shaw means to reminds us that his play is composed of historical events and personages, all freely interpreted. The action is set in XXXIII Dynasty of Egypt, October 48 to March 47 B.C. The chief sources of the play are Shaw's reading in the ancient historian Plutarch, in Shakespeare's *Julius Caesar* and *Antony and Cleopatra*, and in a nineteenth century account of Rome by the German historian, Mommsen. In addition, there is his own thinking about the characters and events, especially as they are depicted in Shakespeare's Roman history play. It is generally agreed that Shaw makes his characters talk not like their originals (whatever they may have been like) but more like advanced thinkers of his own time. Indeed, the character of Caesar has sometimes been identified with Shaw himself.

CHARACTERS

Julius Caesar

The general, statesman, writer; fifty-two, yet still feared and celebrated.

Cleopatra

Not yet the beautiful Queen of legend. Sixteen, an ignorant, childish, willful queen.

Ftatateeta

Cleopatra's nurse, superstitious, vengeful, treacherous.

Pothinus

An Egyptian court adviser, fifty, guardian of Ptolemy and champion of his claims of the throne.

Ptolemy Dionysus

Cleopatra's brother, aged ten.

Britannus

Forty, Caesar's secretary, a captive Briton.

Rufio

A Roman officer given authority by Caesar.

Apollodorus

A handsome Sicilian of twenty-four.

Lucius Septimius

Another Roman officer.

Belzanor

The veteran captain of the guard at the palace in Syria.

Theodotus

The elderly tutor of Ptolemy.

Achillas

Thirty-five, leader of Ptolemy's troops.

Bel Affris

New in the guard at the temple of Ra.

Charmian

One of Cleopatra's handmaidens.

Iras

Another of Cleopatra's favorites. Guards, Sentinels, Soldiers, Musicians, Centurion (a Roman officer), Slaves, Ladies of the Court.

PREFACE

Preface (part of the preface to the *Three Plays for Puritans*). More than half of this preface is a description and criticism of the theatre and public of Shaw's time. Shaw objects mainly to the circumstance that has led the managers to place all their resources at the service of but one kind of play, that which treats sexual infatuation romantically and unrealistically, calling it love, and that teaches the audience to celebrate sensuous ecstasy as the supreme emotion. Shaw says such plays bore him and often lose money for their producers, who pretend to scorn the new drama that is telling the truth about human relations. Thus he prefers, he says, to be a Puritan of a new kind, offering plays in which some such truth is depicted. His purpose in the theatre, he says, is serious, not frivolous, and he has no use for any art whose message is the glorification of sensuality at the expense of will and intellectual striving.

As for *Caesar and Cleopatra*, Shaw thinks it an improvement upon Shakespeare's depiction of the two historical characters. In *Antony and Cleopatra*, Shakespeare spoiled a realistic portrayal of two people going to their ruin through sensuality by trying to make their passion seem heroic at the end. Caesar, too, is not a convincing character in Shakespeare: He is a failure because Shakespeare did not know how to portray a Caesar of strength.

Shaw refuses to be distressed by the outcries of what he calls "Bardolaters," those people who pretend to worship Shakespeare (the Bard) in all his faults, as well as virtues, and who will tolerate no criticism of him, though they will, as Shaw demonstrates, not protect unsatisfactory productions of his plays. Shaw says that the craft of playwriting has not advanced much since Shakespeare's time, so that his craftsmanship cannot be equaled. But there are new ideas and philosophies to be reckoned with and in this respect, not in respect to craft, Shaw claims he has made an advance on Shakespeare. He has written plays with an outlook on life different from that of Shakespeare's time, just as he has benefited from more recent interpretations of Caesar. His originality, he argues, is simply in approaching old material in a new way.

Comment

This preface is important for an understanding of Shaw's criticism of the theatre of his time. Beyond that, it provides a statement of his purposes and beliefs. Note his use of "Puritan." He does not think of the word "Puritan" as meaning rigorous joy-killer and life-denier. Rather, as a Puritan he wants to purify his audience's minds of the foolish and thoughtless illusions about existence and human relations that often pass for acceptable drama.

PROLOGUE

Doorway of the temple of Ra, god of the sun.

From great darkness, and visible by his own light, the Egyptian god Ra speaks to the modern audience. He addresses its members contemptuously as he explains that he has come to take them back two thousand years to a time when there were two Romes, an old and a new, and men were undecided in their allegiance, caught between them. The old Rome was small-minded, aggressive, warlike, on the verge of civil war between the soldier class (led by Pompey the Great) and the new breed of politicians (led by the shrewd Julius Caesar, who had the gods on his side and took initiative and action instead of pleading outworn law and duty, as Pompey continually did). In the strife that followed, Caesar, after what looked like defeat at the hands of the old Rome, won the battle of Pharsalia (48 B.C.). Pompey fled to Egypt, Caesar pursued. The Egyptians did not know which Rome to welcome, Pompey's or Caesar's, and fearful of choosing a loser, consulted Lucius Septimius, a former officer of Pompey promising him rewards if he would give them the answer. He did, and himself stabbed Pompey. As for Cleopatra, she is only a child when all of this happens. Looking for Pompey, Caesar finds her, and this play tells what happened between them, before Caesar left Egypt to fight his way back to Rome and be killed there himself. This is the principal action of the play, says Ra, and the audience will marvel at the fact that men in ancient times are just as they are now: no worse, no better. To a god, 20 centuries is a moment; it is his nature to try to enlighten even the ignorant and the dull. He warns the audience not to applaud him, and leaves.

Comment

This prologue was written by Shaw in 1912 and is not usually performed. It is undramatic, a long monologue, its tone satirical and anti-heroic in its remarks on the modern theatregoers and the smallness of the present century.

AN ALTERNATIVE TO THE PROLOGUE-SETTING

The courtyard of a palace on the Syrian border of Egypt, October, 48 B.C. Night.

At Cleopatra's palace the captain of the guard, Belzanor, is rolling dice with one of the soldiers, known as the Persian. The sentinel allows Bel Affris to enter, who reports that Caesar and his legions are coming closer by the minute. He gives an account of events at the temple of Ra, from where he has just come: Pompey has been slain and the temple guard has been vanquished by the Romans. Excitedly they now consider what to do with Cleopatra, who is supposedly in the palace and must be saved from the advancing enemy and from the treachery of her brother Ptolemy. The Persian proposes a wily scheme that will make *Caesar and Cleopatra* rulers of Egypt, but is interrupted by the mobs of women fleeing the palace. The Queen's nurse Ftatateeta enters, and when questioned about Cleopatra, says she does not know where the girl is. Belzanor and the Persian threaten her until she tells them that Cleopatra is most likely to be found in the desert at the Sphinx to whom she confides all her fears and secrets. Then she trips up the Persian and runs off, as the sentinel cries that the sacred white cat belonging to the priest has been stolen. Panic follows and all rush off.

Comment

This alternative prologue more properly constitutes a dramatic action. It introduces the superstitious court of Cleopatra, creates suspenseful anticipation of the Romans and Caesar, tells us some of the necessary historical information (e.g., the rivalry of Cleopatra and her brother, the murder of Pompey), and sets up the first act, which will take place at the Sphinx.

ACT I

Setting

In the desert, before the Sphinx. Night.

The atmosphere is strangely magical, misty and then radiant with moonlight, and unseen music can be heard. A man enters and stops before the Sphinx, which he proceeds to address. He is Julius Caesar, and he greets the Sphinx as one like himself, a stranger to men and not truly part of this world, both of them having strayed from the region of the ideal where they belong. Caesar recognizes in the Sphinx the "immortal part" of his life to which his destiny has led him and says he is not a man at all but a combination of woman, brute, and god. Suddenly a voice calls to Caesar from the Sphinx, a girl's voice, urging him to climb up on the Sphinx to where she is and so hide from the Romans. She tells him she is Cleopatra, the Queen, who has lost her sacred white cat and who will one day kill her brother Ptolemy and live in the palace at Alexandria. She describes the Romans to him, and not realizing to whom she is talking, pictures Caesar as a barbarian who will eat her once he finds her. But Caesar tells her he will teach her how to avoid being eaten: She must face the Roman leader as a brave woman and queen and then he will make her ruler of Egypt. But she is not convinced and wants to find magical stratagems to overcome him. Caesar calls her a little fool and starts to walk away, but she implores him to take her with him.

The sound of Caesar's approaching legions is heard as the setting changes to the throne room in the palace. These Caesar tell Cleopatra to take her throne and to order her servants to attend her. Ftatateeta, who now comes in, demands to know who Caesar is and is reprimanded by him for daring to question the Queen. In fact, he threatens to leave Cleopatra if she does not command, instead of beseech, her servant. After a show of power that amazes Cleopatra, Ftatateeta is put down by Caesar and the Queen delightedly promises to make him a king to keep him with her. Only one thing worries her, and she asks the man she calls Old Gentleman how she can convince Caesar she is truly a queen. He repeats his instructions to be brave and, dressed in her robes, she tries feebly. A sentinel rushes in to announce Romans in the courtyard! Trumpets sound, men approach, Cleopatra wants to run away until Ftatateeta reminds her she has just said she will be brave and queenly to the end. Caesar leads her back to the throne. Soldiers enter, and seeing their general, hail Caesar. Then Cleopatra understands what has happened and to whom she has been talking, and sobbing with relief falls into Caesar's arms.

Comment

This first act gives us an excellent example of the use of dramatic **irony**. It is constructed on a principle that allows the audience to know what Cleopatra does not, that she is revealing herself to the very man she fears. The suspense is beautifully maintained, and the comedy of Caesar's giving her instruction about behavior before Caesar, testing her at the same time, is neatly developed to the **climax** of the last moments. Note the character of Cleopatra: childish, cruel, ignorant, and yet fascinating. Caesar says she will be his most dangerous conquest and that he is easily deceived by women because he sees them not as they are but as he wants them to be. Caesar's address to the Sphinx is important too. It establishes this leader of men as a romantic and mystic believer in a destiny that will carry him beyond the nightmare of Roman politics and conquests and toward a higher reality he says is not known by ordinary men and is shared by him and the Sphinx.

ACT II

Setting

A hall in Ptolemy's palace at Alexandria.

Prompted by his guardian Pothinus, the boy king Ptolemy reviews the treachery of his sister Cleopatra's claims to the throne and reasserts that with or without Caesar to support her, he, Ptolemy, is King of Egypt. Rufio, the Roman aide, announces the entrance of Caesar, who comes in with Britannus, his secretary, and treats the Egyptians in a friendly and yet firm manner. He astonishes them by reporting he has had his officers collect taxes among the people because he is in need of money, in return for which he is prepared to settle the rival claims to the throne. Now he has Cleopatra brought in, who is unruly until controlled by Caesar. When he hears that Ptolemy and Cleopatra are considered husband and wife as well as brother and sister-Britannus is scandalized by this-he proposes to let them reign jointly. But Pothinus and the others want Caesar to leave them to settle their own affairs. They remind him of the dissention among the Roman forces, and it takes the appearance of his soldiers in the building to show them which Roman rules here, Caesar or Achillas, the general left by Pompey. He urges Pothinus and his friends to leave the palace while they may. Their answer is to call in Lucius Septimius, who recalls to the remorseful Caesar the strategic murder of Pompey and other enemies of Rome. Caesar regrets all of this now, pleading that he was a different man then and a lesser one. Then they leave, and Rufio chides Caesar for his leniency with enemies.

With his permission Cleopatra now takes firm charge of the palace household. To his dismay she threatens those who serve her and tries to patronize even Caesar. She tells him of the handsome soldier she loves, who saved her father's kingdom years before, and when Caesar reveals that it was he who sent this young man, Mark Antony, she is grateful to him. After she has left, Caesar sits down to work but is prevented by a wounded soldier coming in to tell him that Achillas and the other Egyptians Caesar released have attacked the Romans and besieged them. Caesar gives Rufio orders to seize the lighthouse on the island of Pharos after burning the Roman ships in the west harbor. Pothinus enters with an ultimatum demanding that Caesar leave. But Caesar declares him a prisoner, just as Theodotus, the old tutor, comes in to report that the precious library has caught fire. To this Caesar is indifferent, and says the shameful records of the past ought to be burned because they seduce and flatter mankind with false illusions. Let the past burn-live for the future! All the same, he gives permission to have Achillas' legions help to put out the fire and orders Pothinus to go with Theodotus. The legions are now embarked, and Cleopatra helps Caesar on with his armor and begs him to come back when it is safe to do so. Rufio, seeing the Egyptian army on the edge of the west harbor, curses Caesar's leniency, until he realizes they are there to put out the fire in the library, set by Caesar's orders and shrewd strategy. And so, under this diversion Caesar steps aboard his galley and makes for the lighthouse.

Comment

Caesar controls this act. He is calm and self-possessed in his dealings with the renegade army of occupation and its Egyptian leaders. And our attention is on him in the crucial confrontation with Septimius in which he confesses the mistakes of his past, condemning his resort then to political murder. This regret is neatly balanced by the scene in which he wishes to let the past be symbolically destroyed in the library fire. And at the end we see his courageous braving of Pothinus, when he knows his forces are outnumbered by Ptolemy's, and then under the appearance of idealism, his clever deployment of the Egyptian troops to the fire while he makes his retreat to Pharos.

ACT III

Setting

The wharf outside the palace. Later the lighthouse on a peninsula leading to the harbor of Alexandria.

This act is divided into two scenes, the first of which takes place on the wharf where the Sicilian Apollodorus is attempting to get past a sentinel with Ftatateeta and a pile of rugs for the Queen. After a skirmish with the guard, a centurion allows them to pass. Cleopatra comes to them from the palace and demands a boat to row her out to the lighthouse and to Caesar. This brings a fresh outbreak of fighting between Apollodorus and the guard, who has his orders not to let anyone out of the palace. Again the centurion restores calm. Cleopatra inquires of Apollodorus about sending a rug to Caesar, then retires to the palace with her nurse. Soon after a rug is brought down to the wharfside and placed in a boat, with instructions by Ftatateeta to handle it carefully. As the boat leaves the shore, the guard realizes from the old woman's prayer that somehow Cleopatra is in the boat too.

The scene changes to the lighthouse of Pharos, where Rufio sits eating outside the door below the tower. Caesar enters, concerned about a fresh attack and possible defeat by the Egyptians, and Rufio tries to cheer him. Britannus comes in with captured documents giving the names of Roman traitors in Pompey's army, but Caesar will have nothing to do with political vengeance and orders them burned. Britannus rebukes him for not taking things seriously, as all respectable Britons do. Apollodorus comes in with news of his gift from Cleopatra. Caesar gives orders to have it hoisted by crane, and Apollodorus mounts the chain jauntily and is drawn up astride the rug. When it reaches the platform, the bundle is undone, and Cleopatra steps out of the rolled up rug and stands before a pleased Caesar, an angry Rufio, and a shocked Britannus. But Caesar is concerned for her safety and orders Apollodorus to return her to Alexandria. A sudden tumult now. The Egyptian forces have attacked and cut off the lighthouse from the protecting barricade there, trapping the Roman forces between shore and land and leaving Caesar and his party stranded at the lighthouse. Quick decisions have to be made. Apollodorus finds a solution. He offers to swim to the east harbor and send a rescuing galley. Then he leaps into the sea, and a moment later Rufio seizes the resisting Cleopatra and throws her into the harbor after him. Britannus will not budge, but Caesar promises to swim too and recapture the lighthouse. The day is saved.

Comment

This act is filled with melodramatics, with adventurous and even sensational moments-Apollodorus dueling with the sentinel, the hoisting of Cleopatra in the rug, the leap into the sea. The **themes** of the play are not much advanced, though there is Caesar's refusal to take revenge on his opponents. Note the character of Apollodorus: he is young, handsome, brave, a storybook hero with a sense of dashing humor and apparent disregard for his safety. Contrast Britannus, who is meant as a caricature of the respectable Englishman of later times. He is cautious, easily shocked by the improper, and concerned for appearances and public opinion. And he is dependable and faithful to Caesar, who repays him with affection just as he repays Rufio's loyalty by treating him as a son.

ACT IV

Setting

Cleopatra's boudoir in the palace. Then a roof garden. 47 B.C., nearly five months later.

Surrounded by her women, Cleopatra listens impatiently to their chatter. She seems changed, much more serious now, and desires to be a Queen who is obeyed. She praises Caesar for teaching her about people and will hear no idle criticism of him. Pothinus has bribed Ftatateeta to allow him an interview with the Queen and now enters. He remarks on the change in Cleopatra, too, and she explains to him that Caesar has made her wiser, has taught her to be concerned not with her personal happiness but with the things that must be done to govern well. Caesar does not love her, she says, and his care for her he would extend to anyone because it is his nature to be kind. Besides, he is a god to her, above love. Pothinus warns her that his forces will eventually drive Caesar from Egypt, but Cleopatra is not convinced and leaves him. He stays behind to exchange some words with Ftatateeta, warning her that Egypt will never tolerate a Roman-hearted queen and she will never rule while he lives.

On the roof garden of the palace, where a banquet is being laid, Caesar speaks with Rufio about the dangerous behavior of Pothinus. But Pothinus himself enters and informs Caesar that Cleopatra is a traitor. He has no time to make good his charges, for the Queen enters now, angry at seeing him with Caesar. Caesar cleverly offers to let him leave unmolested, but Pothinus prefers to stay and accuse Cleopatra directly of wanting Caesar's departure so that she may rule Egypt alone once he has secured the throne for her from Ptolemy. Caesar believes him, but is unimpressed by the information. He finds it natural, he tells Cleopatra, that she should want him out of the way and be ambitious for herself, and he is not resentful. He then escorts Pothinus past the guard, going out with Rufio and leaving the Queen and Ftatateeta. Smoldering, Cleopatra orders her nurse to see that Pothinus does not leave the palace alive. The nurse goes out, and Caesar comes back with Rufio and Apollodorus.

At the banquet Caesar is relaxed and thoughtful. He wants to leave Rome behind in all its corrupted greatness and build a holy city for Cleopatra in some unknown region. Cleopatra offers to invoke the spirit of the Nile to name the city, and a priest enters to perform a sacred ceremony. Cleopatra says a sacrifice is needed, but will not say what. Suddenly a cry is heard, and Caesar, glancing at Cleopatra, knows from her eyes that someone has been killed. Ftatateeta comes in, and Cleopatra embraces her, but at Caesar's order is sent away again, followed by Rufio. Caesar questions Cleopatra, who denies she is hiding anything. But Apollodorus and Britannus come in with Lucius Septimius, and the truth is out. Pothinus has been murdered and the city is in an uproar. Caesar is appalled, Cleopatra triumphant at having revenged herself on an enemy who would have betrayed them both. She asks all but Caesar in turn if she was right in having Pothinus murdered, and all, in some measure, agree. Now Caesar turns on them, the verdict against him, and explains passionately that their idea of retribution is base because one vengeance leads to another, without end, and murder breeds murder in the name of supposedly right ideals. Perhaps the gods will one day tire of it and create an enlightened race. In the meanwhile Caesar says he will give up Egypt's defense and let Cleopatra solve her problems herself. Now Cleopatra is frightened and implores him not to desert her, and the others plead military necessities. Even Caesar appears alarmed, for the Romans are outnumbered and the Egyptians may easily avenge Pothinus' death. Septimius now saves them. In return for his life and a command in Caesar's army, he offers a piece of good news. But Caesar anticipates him: A relief army is on its way. Caesar immediately makes plans to join his forces with it and sends out Lucius and Rufio; he then prepares to fight, after promising Cleopatra to settle her affairs later. After he leaves, Rufio realizes from Cleopatra's boast that the murderer of Pothinus is Ftatateeta, now praying at the altar of Ra. He pretends to go out, and a moment later Cleopatra calls the nurse to her. When she does not come, the Queen goes to the altar - and there finds Ftatateeta with her throat cut.

Comment

The **climax** of the play is the murder of Pothinus and the repudiation of it by Caesar. He is called a dreamer by some of the others and impractical, but in his speech on the futility of vengeance he shows he is more of a realist than the practical people. He is not only a soldier, but as Apollodorus says, a "creative poet-artist" in his vision of a holy city uncontaminated by human wickedness. He has tried to teach Cleopatra to be moral, but she is savage, a dangerous kitten, and while she appreciates the force of his example, she cannot in a crisis do as Caesar does. She knows only the ways of retaliation and revenge. It is part of the comedy of the play that Caesar is practical in another sense. He may be an idealist who is saddened by the world, but he knows how to deal with people, to act in an emergency, to form and pursue a strategy.

ACT V

Setting

The esplanade before the palace. Noon. There is a holiday mood in the city following Caesar's victory over Achillas and the renegade forces, a victory now reviewed by Apollodorus and Belzanor. Caesar arrives on the esplanade, ready to board his galley and leave for Rome. But first he appoints Rufio governor, offers freedom to Britannus, who graciously refuses it to remain with Caesar, and then minimizes the importance of possible death if he goes to Rome without the protection Rufio offers him. He is about to board his ship when Cleopatra enters, simply and beautifully dressed. Caesar assures her Rufio will rule in Caesar's way, without punishment, revenge, or judgment, and Cleopatra tests his word by declaring Rufio the murderer of Ftatateeta. But Caesar excuses the murder as having been done without malice or in the name of some empty virtue.

Cleopatra now seems reconciled. Caesar promises her a gift from Rome, one of the greatest it can bestow: one of her sons, Mark Antony. Then he kisses her farewell, saying he thinks they will not meet again. She is crying as she waves goodbye to Caesar, and the soldiers hail him as his ship draws away.

Comment

In this short closing act, Caesar leaves Cleopatra but leaves behind, hopefully, all he has tried to teach her. The future belongs to her and to Mark Antony. Caesar does not know, as Shaw does and we do, the unhappy outcome of their meeting; meanwhile, Caesar has done what he can to make Cleopatra a humane woman and Queen by giving her a lesson in practicality and idealism. History tells us that Caesar returned to Rome and, as Rufio feared, to his death (assassinated in 44 B.C.).

Note

Shaw follows the play with a few pages of notes on his characters and themes. The most important section is possibly that on the character of Caesar, for which see material immediately following.

ANALYSIS OF SELECTED CHARACTERS

Caesar

Shaw says that he has attributed originality and natural greatness to his hero. By nature Caesar is above resentment, too great to need to forgive anyone or to be less than completely honest. He is above generosity, because he acknowledges openly that he makes use of people and will not demean them by expecting gratitude. Because he has virtue, says Shaw, he has "no need of goodness," that complacent urge to self-denial that passes commonly for virtue. His ambition is to make the world better and men more truly civilized. He is on his way to being a master of reality (see below, *Man and Superman*, for a discussion of this phrase); he is a man who desires to make a holy city free of corruption from self-deceived and vicious humanity. All in one, he is a realist, idealist, dreamer, artist, genius.

Cleopatra

She is Caesar's pupil and their relations are not sexual. Caesar knows she is uncivilized in his sense and does not trust her. But he is open with her and helps her to become ruler of Egypt, as much for reasons of Roman policy as out of liking for her. In Act IV she goes back on the lessons he tries to teach her and reverts to savage vengeance on Pothinus. But in the last act she is sober and dignified again, tearful at seeing Caesar depart and yet able to say that she hopes he will not return. He is really too much for her. He continually astonishes her by the mixture in him of shrewdness and apparent unconcern for his welfare and by his ability to make her feel ashamed of her pettiness. In short, she admires and fears him.

Britannus

A character who is comic in his inflexibility. Shaw intends him as a joke on the ordinary middle-class Englishman who thinks his country and its customs superior to any in the world. He is easily shocked and is always concerned for propriety.

Notice his advice to Caesar when they are about to leap from the lighthouse in Act III. He urges Caesar not to be seen in Alexandria before he has changed his clothes. Such advice is comically out of place at such a moment. But Britannus is not only a comic foil. Through him we see Caesar's humanity, his kindness to people of all sorts and abilities. When he offers Britannus his freedom, the secretary's response is touching: "Only as Caesar's slave have I found real freedom."

ESSAY QUESTIONS AND ANSWERS

Question: Is *Caesar and Cleopatra* historically true?

Answer: It is true that in October, 47 B.C., Julius Caesar came to Egypt in pursuit of Pompey, once his friend, later his enemy, whom he had just defeated at the battle of Pharsalia. He found that Pompey was already dead. He stayed for half a year and established Cleopatra firmly as queen of Egypt. These are the historical facts that George Bernard Shaw uses in his play.

All the other material in the play is not historically true. Some of it is actually known to be untrue. Much of it comes straight from Shaw's imagination, and we have no way of knowing whether he is right or wrong.

One important fact which Shaw alters is Cleopatra's age. He makes her sixteen, an age he sees as balanced between childhood and womanhood. He tips the scales by giving her an exceptionally immature nature, so that in every way she is very much a child, with the single exception of her outspoken sexual interest in Mark Antony. But Cleopatra was twenty-one when Caesar came, for evidence indicates that she was born in 69 B.C. By no stretch of the imagination can a twenty-one-year-old girl be considered a child. It was necessary for Shaw to reduce her age for the purposes of the play. Otherwise, he could not keep the sexual element out of her relationship with Caesar; nor could he show her in such an undeveloped state that Caesar could easily influence her.

Historical evidence strongly suggests that Caesar and Cleopatra did have a sexual relationship. The fact that Cleopatra had a son whom she named Ptolemy Caesar (his nickname was Caesarion, "small Caesar") and for whom she claimed Julius Caesar as father seems sufficient proof, though Caesar did not acknowledge the child as his. But Shaw wishes to escape from this in his play, not because he disapproves of sexual passion (he does not) but because sexual passion is a boring **cliche** on the stage and he wants to write about something else.

In other, smaller ways Shaw goes against historical fact. For example, the death in Rome of Vercingetorix, the Gallic general, is spoken of, although it did not actually take place until after Caesar left Egypt and returned to Rome. As another example, Shaw gives a strong impression at the end of the play that Cleopatra and Caesar will never meet again. She actually followed him to Rome and lived there until Caesar's death by assassination in 44 B.C.

Many of the characters and events in the play are the products of Shaw's imagination. Ftatateeta, Rufio, Britannus are all Shaw's creations. It is delightful to think that Caesar saw Cleopatra when he came to look at the Sphinx by moonlight and found her hiding from the Romans between its great stone paws-but it does not seem very likely. The same is true of many other striking episodes.

To sum up, Shaw is not a historian but a creative artist. We do not read *Caesar and Cleopatra* to learn facts, but to enjoy satisfaction of our intellects and imaginations. Though based on a real meeting between the two main characters, Shaw's account of a brilliant, sophisticated Caesar trying to educate a headstrong, violent young Egyptian queen is his own invention.

Question: Discuss the importance of the settings in *Caesar and Cleopatra*.

Answer: The love of spectacle is present in every audience. Today, audiences tend to satisfy their love of spectacle at the movies. The movies are perfect for showing magnificent effects, and in our time, films show us beautiful scenery, great mansions and ballrooms, huge battles, and "casts of thousands." But in the nineteenth century, spectacular effects were to be found on the stage. Plays with great crowds, gorgeous costumes, sinking ships, and other such devices were almost always popular. This was one reason why there were many historical plays, for historical events gave the best excuse for spectacular scenes.

There was only one trouble with these plays: like modern movie spectacles, they were nice to look at but uninteresting or plain silly to listen to. Shaw decided to take advantage of the popular interest in spectacles. But he wrote a play that was a pleasure to the mind as well as the eye. The fact that there was so much to see perhaps helped to make the unusual ideas in the play less disturbing.

Caesar and Cleopatra is an ever-changing, always colorful panorama on the stage. There are nine scenes, and only two of them have the same setting. Each scene uses much lavish display and many characters. In the last scene, Caesar's ship actually moves.

But Shaw gets more than spectacular value out of the backgrounds. Often they contribute to the power of a scene. The most impressive example is the end of the fourth act; as time passes, the light changes and fades until it is night. The great altar of Ra in the background is strange and threatening. The last great effect-that of Ftatateeta lying dead on Ra's altar in the moonlight-is entirely visual.

To sum up, in *Caesar and Cleopatra*, Shaw takes advantage of his audience's love of spectacle to make his play acceptable. But he also makes the physical setting of the play contribute to the effective expression of his ideas.

Question: Examine the relationship between Caesar and Cleopatra

Answer: Shaw shows the Roman conqueror and the Egyptian queen in what to him is the most interesting of human relationships-that of teacher and pupil. We do not often stop to think about it, but this relationship (which exists in many places besides in school) is the instrument of our humanity. It is the way we make available to new generations what we have already discovered, so that the new generation does not have to learn everything all over again by trial, error, and failure. By her six-month association with Caesar, Cleopatra learns more about being a queen than she could learn in a lifetime by her own efforts.

Caesar is an extraordinary human being. In his lifetime he has learned a great deal about men and their relationships with one another because of his unusual powers of observation and understanding. He has what Shaw calls "an original mind." He sees things for himself and acts according to what he sees, rather than according to what other people assume to be right. Therefore his treatment of his enemies, his behavior toward his followers, even his military strategy-all are exceptionally effective even though unusual.

Cleopatra herself is only sixteen years old, but she is capable of learning from her observation of reality. As she sees Caesar get devotion from his servants and soldiers, respect from his enemies, and victory in war, she is able to understand how this is done. She learns the advantages of avoiding unnecessary violence-even in war, for Caesar holds off a huge Egyptian army entirely by being careful not to arouse any real antagonism in its members. She learns about the strength that is so sure of itself that it can afford to relax and be kind.

Cleopatra changes because of what Caesar teaches her. The ignorant, silly little barbarian of the first act becomes more sophisticated, more restrained. She takes on queenly dignity, though this takes a while. In Act II she still sticks out her tongue at her brother. She learns that a queen does what must be done, not what she wants to do. These are some examples of what she comes to understand through her association with Caesar.

But the relationship is more complicated than this. Caesar is a great man, but Cleopatra is not a great woman. There is much viciousness in her character. No amount of good example can take away her enjoyment of suffering or her cruel indifference to anyone's fate but her own. Also, she remains self-willed, ambitious, calculating, and sensual. In short, though she understands Caesar's great qualities, she has only a limited ability to imitate them herself, as a result of her own very imperfect nature.

There is no sexual love between them. On Cleopatra's side there are gratitude and admiration, but she cannot love a god. Or, in other words, she is made uncomfortable by this man who is not thrown off balance by the human emotions of anger and love. Caesar, on the other hand, does not love any one person. He pours out kindness indiscriminately on slaves and queens, but because he is a unique genius (as he himself tells the Sphinx when the play opens) he does not need anybody. Where there is no need, there is no love.

To sum up, between wise, tolerant Caesar and the violent, selfish girl queen, there is the bond that exists between master and pupil, but there is no emotional involvement. Shaw demonstrates here that it is possible to have a significant human relationship that does not have emotion as its basis.

Question: Explain Shaw's use of the **theme** of vengeance in this play.

Answer: Caesar is disgusted by the taking of vengeance. That vengeance is wrong is his most characteristic idea. None of the other characters shares it. Rufio and Britannus are mentally incapable of seeing what he means. Cleopatra is not able to control her anger and follow Caesar's teaching when someone injures her.

The **theme** is introduced in the second act. Pothinus and Theodotus demand gratitude from Caesar because they ordered the murder of Pompey, his enemy. They call as witness Lucius Septimius, who actually did the killing. Caesar can hardly bear to look at Lucius Septimius. Instead of being grateful because they helped him get revenge on Pompey, he lashes out at them. They are astonished. He reminds them that even though Pompey became his enemy, once he was the husband of Caesar's own daughter. He remembers his friendship with Pompey, and Pompey's many services to Rome. Only a savage beast would rejoice at receiving a present of an old friend's head. Lucius Septimius replies that Caesar himself has killed and mutilated many enemies. Caesar then becomes ashamed of his wrath; he admits that he has done such things, though he would not do them now. He apologizes to Lucius Septimius.

In Act IV the **theme** of vengeance is introduced again, further developed, and brought to its **climax**. Lucius Septimius is again the symbol of vengeance. He comes to announce Pothinus' death and to accuse Caesar of arranging it. At length, Cleopatra admits that she ordered Pothinus killed. She asks each person present to judge whether she was wrong. Their reasons differ slightly, but they all agree that she is right and Caesar is wrong.

Never has Caesar's isolation been brought home to him so painfully. He eloquently explains the futility of revenge as he sees it-how each injury calls forth another injury in revenge, and that one calls forth still another, and so on endlessly. Humanity creates a perpetual bloodbath in the name of peace and justice. The man who really understands this, says Caesar, must either conquer the world-or be crucified by it!

In a practical sense, Caesar is soon proved correct, because Pothinus' murder puts all their own lives in danger. Only the arrival of reinforcements saves them.

The outcome of Pothinus' murder is another murder, just as Caesar foretold. To protect Caesar from her, Rufio kills Ftatateeta, who killed Pothinus.

To sum up, Caesar's understanding of the futility of revenge proves his greatness. His most splendid and lonely moment is when he defends this idea against the other characters after the death of Pothinus.

Question: How does Shaw feel about Shakespeare's plays about *Caesar and Cleopatra*?

Answer: Shaw explains in his preface that his dissatisfaction with Shakespeare's handling of these characters is one reason why he wrote *Caesar and Cleopatra*. In Shakespeare, they do not appear in the same play. *Antony and Cleopatra* shows a mature Cleopatra who gives everything for the love of Mark Antony. Shaw claims that Shakespeare demonstrates what a vulgar sexual infatuation exists between them, and how they are self-indulgent and irresponsible because of it. (Lovers of this type, says Shaw, can be found in any bar.) But then Shakespeare makes them glamorous and tragic instead of simply sordid. This makes the play false and therefore unsatisfying.

Shakespeare's *Julius Caesar* appears in the play of the same name. Shakespeare portrays him as foolish and conceited. This is a misrepresentation of a great man, and Shaw wants to correct it with his own interpretation.

Shaw intends to present a Cleopatra who is not simply a romantic temptress and a Caesar who is a convincingly great man. Furthermore, his play will deal with a human relationship that involves something else besides sexual passion.

Outside of these points, Shaw realizes that his plays are not the equal of Shakespeare's. Shaw's own plays re-examine Shakespeare's characters in the light of new ideas. This is the only special value that he claims for them.

Question: Discuss the portrayals of the secondary characters in *Caesar and Cleopatra*.

Answer: *Caesar and Cleopatra* is a play of great scope, having numerous scenes and many characters. Attention is mainly focused on Caesar and Cleopatra themselves, but there are a number of other characters who are important to the action of the play. These are drawn in some detail. For convenience, they may be divided into those associated with Caesar, those attached to Cleopatra, and those surrounding the young king, Ptolemy.

Rufio, the Roman officer, and Britannus, the secretary, are Caesar's followers.

Rufio is an outspoken, straightforward, practical military man. His father was a freed slave; so Rufio has worked his way into Caesar's confidence by his dependability and energy. His main interest is Caesar's welfare. One characteristic action of his occurs in Act II. When Caesar has no chair in Ptolemy's court, Rufio takes a tripod from before the altar of the god Ra, brushes off the burning incense, and gives it to Caesar to sit on. Rufio does not stop to think it over before taking this action. He is unworried by the insult he has offered to the Egyptian god. Caesar needs a chair and Rufio supplies it simply and promptly. Rufio's concern is so great when Caesar does something dangerous that he uses blunt, sometimes disrespectful language to him. All in all, Rufio well deserves the title of "Caesar's shield"; Caesar calls him this when he says goodbye to him.

Britannus is a slave who was captured by the Romans during Caesar's invasion of Britain. He is now serving as Caesar's secretary. Shaw makes him into a highly comic caricature of the conservative middle-class Englishman. For instance, he is always dressed in blue; this is a satirical reference to the respectable blue suit of the modern Englishman. He is serious in his outlook and pompous in his manner. He has no sense of humor whatever. He finds Caesar too informal and frivolous, but he puts this down to the fact that Caesar is an Italian, not an Englishman. His love for Caesar is as great as Rufio's. He devotes himself wholeheartedly to Caesar's service.

Cleopatra's chief servant is her nurse, Ftatateeta. She is a large, ugly, elderly woman; while the queen is still a child, she bullies and controls her. Cleopatra matures under Caesar's teaching, and Ftatateeta becomes her fiercely devoted servant. She loves Cleopatra almost as if she were her child. She feels personally responsible for Cleopatra's actions; for example, if Cleopatra gives her word, Ftatateeta sees to it that she keeps it. Ftatateeta will do anything for Cleopatra. She kills Pothinus at the queen's command-and enjoys it. Shaw paints her as a combination of savagery and devotion.

Apollodorus becomes a supporter of Cleopatra early in the play. His courage, gallantry and courtesy attract her to him. He in turn is glad to offer his assistance, whether it be in her childish scheme to visit Caesar rolled inside a carpet, or in her defense when she admits she is responsible for Pothinus' death. (We must also note that, in the crucial moment when Caesar plans to break out of the palace and go to meet his reinforcements at the Nile Delta, Apollodorus goes off with Caesar and leaves Cleopatra alone.) Even though Apollodorus is dashing and charming, he is a rather shallow character compared to Caesar. While Caesar deals with the realities of war and peace, Apollodorus is mainly concerned with ornamental things.

The boy king Ptolemy is surrounded by such followers as Pothinus, Achillas, and Theodotus.

The king himself is an appealing child. He is a hapless pawn in the struggle for power in Egypt. He responds shyly but warmly to Caesar's friendliness. He leaves an impression of loneliness and bravery. His relations with Cleopatra are the normal quarreling ones between children in the same family.

Pothinus, the king's tutor, is an unprincipled, intriguing politician who hopes to use the boy as an instrument in his own climb to power. He intends to be the man behind the throne. He cares nothing for Ptolemy himself. His inability to control his emotions leads to disaster. Pothinus comes to Caesar privately to reveal to him that Cleopatra is planning her own rise to power when Caesar leaves. Caesar shows little interest in Pothinus' secret. Pothinus is so infuriated that he tells it in front of Cleopatra. Cleopatra's anger can then only be satisfied by Pothinus' death.

Achillas, the commander of the Egyptian army, is portrayed as a strong, forceful man. He is a complete opportunist, using his army as a weapon, not for any particular government or principle, but for his own interest.

The learned Theodotus is the king's tutor. He is a cruel little man. With malicious pleasure he tells how Pompey was beheaded when he came to Egypt. All the love and loyalty he has are devoted to the world of learning. Though he cares little about death and suffering in men, he is heartbroken when the library of Alexandria catches fire.

Question: Why are there two different openings to this play? Compare them.

Answer: The original opening scene of the play is the one now described as "An alternative to the Prologue." It is set in the courtyard of Cleopatra's palace near the Syrian border. Like all opening scenes, its main purposes is to make clear whatever information is needed for the audience to understand the action of the play. This is done here by conversation among the soldiers. Bel Affris brings the news of Caesar's arrival. As he answers the eager questions of the other soldiers, he gives a picture of how terrible the Romans are in battle. Ftatateeta explains to the soldiers how Cleopatra has run away after being scolded. From this we understand that Cleopatra is like a child in her behavior. The scene is full of the activity of soldiers and the hysteria of the palace women. It is lively and interesting.

However, although this scene does its work of explanation well, and though it is also theatrically effective, it has a certain practical disadvantage. The body of the play has eight separate scenes, each one spectacular, and only two scenes are in the same place. Thus seven expensive settings have to be provided for the production. This scene adds an eighth setting. Also, the play is long. This elaborate opening scene makes it even longer.

The scene we now call the Prologue was written by Shaw in 1912 to take the place of the one just discussed. It solves the problems created by the other scene. It is both shorter and simpler. Its sole character is the Egyptian god Ra. The setting is the entrance to Ra's temple. The scene consists of a monologue by Ra, in which he reviews the story of Pompey and Caesar and also provides whatever other information the audience will need. His speech is most amusing; Ra strikes out wittily at the shortcomings of the modern audience he is addressing.

The only trouble is that Ra's speech is a history lecture; no amount of wit can disguise that fact. This is a static scene. Nothing happens in it. For these reasons it is not appealing to a theater audience, even though it is pleasant and stimulating to read.

We may summarize by saying that Shaw's original opening scene is lively and colorful, but adds considerably to the length and cost of the production, while the scene he wrote later is economical in setting and moderate in length but not as effective as the first one.

Question: How does Caesar illustrate Shaw's idea of greatness?

Answer: According to Shaw, the most important sign of human greatness is originality of mind. That is, a great man will not think or do what everybody else thinks or does. His actions will depend on his own direct insight, not on what is expected of him. He will not be controlled even by other people's conventional ideas of right and wrong. We know that in life there is the possibility that a man like that will be dangerously ruthless. But in this play, Caesar's natural kindliness is combined with his greatness, so that he turns out to be less cruel than anyone else.

Caesar shows numerous signs of original genius. He permits great familiarity, even rudeness, in his subordinates. He knows that in this way he can be sure they are always honest with him. His soldiers have standing orders to let prisoners escape. This saves the trouble of feeding them and watching them.

The most striking example of Caesar's originality is his hatred of vengeance; to him this is no more than bloodthirstiness disguised as morality. He has a profound understanding, almost religious in character, of the fact that vengeance creates nothing but more vengeance. Humanity will never advance to a higher plane until it gives up revenge, both private and public.

In general, Shaw visualizes Caesar's greatness as the free exercise of Caesar's natural qualities of mind and heart. This makes him tolerant, humorous, intellectually eager, successful in human relations, and brilliant in the exercise of military strategy. Shaw explains that this kind of greatness is quite different from what dramatists usually give to their heroes; most heroes in plays are men who force themselves into conventionally good behavior against their naturally bad instincts.

Question: Does Shaw try to create the atmosphere of ancient times in this play?

Answer: In certain ways, Shaw does give the impression of another age in this play. The settings and costumes are, of course, meant to create the illusion that we are watching Egyptians and Romans in the first century B.C. The dialogue too is made colorful by words and phrases not found in modern speech. "Thee" and "thou" are used instead of "you", especially by the Egyptians, for Shaw intends to make the Egyptians seem more strange and exotic to us than the Romans. Other examples of flavorful language are the appellations tossed back and forth among the porters and boatmen in Act II, such as "Thou mangy dromedary" and "O son of a snail."

These are only occasional ornaments of speech, however. The dialogue is essentially brisk, clear, vivid, and flexible. It represents the best type of modern English speech rather than ancient language.

This is in accordance with Shaw's idea, expressed both in Ra's Prologue and the Notes at the end of the play, that humanity has not changed in any important way in two thousand years. Most people, he states, simply assume that things are getting better all the time, but this is an illusion. It is true that certain details of human environment have changed. Human beings can get from one place to another faster than they used to. Cloth is mass-produced and cheap. But we have made these changes by paying a terrible price in noise, smells, smoke, dirt, ugliness, and overcrowding. And humanity has not changed in the only important way-by increasing its command over itself.

Shaw says that for these reasons he has shown the people in *Caesar and Cleopatra* to be just the same as the people in modern times-with the same weaknesses, the same cruelties, the same possibilities, the same desires. Anyway, this is really the only way he can show them, for these are the only kinds of people he knows and understands.

Question: What are Cleopatra's most important character traits?

Answer: Cleopatra is cruel, self-centered, proud, and vengeful. She is, in fact, a young girl who is not yet completely formed in character, but who possesses the seeds of those destructive qualities that will one day bring her and Mark Antony to ruin. She shows throughout the play a complete lack of regard for soldiers, servants, and other ordinary people. Having been raised in a violent atmosphere, she finds torture and murder a natural solution to any problem. She would gladly kill her little brother if she got the chance; the only excuse for her is that he would just as willingly kill her. All people and events call forth her interest exactly to the extent that they help her or hurt her.

Yet there is a genuine impulse toward learning in her. Within a few months, Caesar teaches her a great deal about being a queen. She understands what it is that makes him so successful in wielding power, even though she is young and inexperienced. Unfortunately, her recklessness and selfishness prevent her from imitating him.

In spite of her imperfect character, Cleopatra has charm, and she already is beginning to understand how to use it. Thus she has an attractiveness on the surface which is contradicted by her basic nature. Caesar is never fooled by her even for a moment.

CRITICAL COMMENTARY

Caesar And Cleopatra

This play is generally considered one of Shaw's masterpieces. Archibald Henderson, the chief authority on Shaw, states that Caesar is Shaw's greatest character portrait, with the exception of *Saint Joan*, in the play of that name.

Henderson points out that with his portrait Bernard Shaw changed the whole concept of how heroes and heroic deeds should be shown. Before this, heroes were portrayed as superhuman; their joys, sufferings, speeches, fighting were all more than life size. They were totally incredible. But Shaw's Caesar is a convincing human being. He is a great man, but he also has his human weaknesses. Henderson states that we see him as if he were in his dressing gown.

Hesketh Pearson remarks, in his biography of Shaw, that Caesar is the most satisfying masculine character in the English drama since Shakespeare. Pearson also mentions regretfully that the portrait is somewhat naive; if all Caesars in real life were like Shaw's Caesar, human history would be much pleasanter. In real life, they turn out to be like Mussolini, Hitler, or Stalin.

Pearson states that *Caesar and Cleopatra* is Shaw's most important work because it had more influence than any other.

From it began the custom of writing about historical characters in a natural manner.

Pearson also makes an interesting identification between Caesar and Shaw himself. He calls Caesar a self-portrait of Shaw.

The British drama critic Desmond MacCarthy discusses *Caesar and Cleopatra* in his book entitled *Shaw*. The discussion is actually a review of a 1913 production of the play. In it MacCarthy expresses doubt that the Caesar in the play is really the Caesar of history. He has the intellect, courage, and generosity of the historical Caesar. But we get an impression of brutal power from the writings of ancient historians; this is lacking in the Caesar in the play. Also. MacCarthy finds it difficult to believe that Caesar had no personal interest in Cleopatra. He concludes that Shaw did not re-create the Caesar of history, but he did create a great man of a different type, so it does not matter.

Almost all critics who discuss the play speak of the power and splendor of the various scenes. The opening scene, with Caesar's beautiful first speech and the superb contrast provided by Cleopatra's words, "Old gentleman!," is singled out for special praise by Archibald Henderson and Hesketh Pearson. C. B. Purdom, in *A Guide to the Plays of Bernard Shaw*, is a minority of one when he says that the play is thinly written.

General Remarks

There has been a great deal of criticism written about the life, work, and thought of George Bernard Shaw. His career was long; he was exposed to criticism for over half a century during his own lifetime, and since his death in 1950 the commentary has continued. There is almost no drama critic who has not had his chance to write something about Bernard Shaw, for productions of Shaw's plays are unceasing. It is surprising that so little of this criticism is really intelligent or enlightening. It is well known that much criticism of Shaw is weak; Eric Bentley remarks upon this in his valuable short book, *Bernard Shaw*.

What are the reasons for this? Why is the criticism of Shaw less intelligent as a whole than the criticism of Shakespeare, for instance, when Shakespeare is a more puzzling and more intricate writer than Shaw?

One reason may well be Shaw's deceptive simplicity. He tries to write his plays very clearly, and often he even goes on to explain his purposes all over again in prefaces. Therefore numerous critics of limited ability are very sure that they understand Shaw. But Shaw is not simple, even though he tries to be clear. In the first place, some of his theories are complicated. It is easy to understand them in a general way, but much harder to absorb all the details. Then too, it may be that Shaw could not explain himself completely. Like many great creative artists, he had certain qualities that he was unaware of himself. Thus, though he could explain what he meant to do, he could not always explain what he actually did do.

A second factor is the anger Shaw arouses in many critics. They are troubled by his ideas and resentful of his self-confident and stinging expression of them. Anger and prejudice do not make a good basis for objective study. (Indeed, it is to be hoped that students will be the superiors of their elders in this. If Shaw expresses an opinion contrary to what a student believes, the student should remain calm, keep his mind open, and respect Shaw's opinion even if he cannot agree with it. This will often happen, for nobody accepts everything Shaw says, and some people accept very little of it. Above all, he should not fail to appreciate Shaw's writing because he happens to be unsympathetic to some of Shaw's thinking.)

Shaw's Ideas

Critical writing about Bernard Shaw usually discusses one or more of the following subjects: his ideas, his talent as a playwright, his writing style, and his life. The reader should try to be aware of any prejudices a critic may have as he reads. This is especially true of discussion about ideas. However, antagonism to Shaw's ideas sometimes affects other discussions, about his plays or his life, for instance.

Shaw's thinking is radical. His ideas on religion, sex, marriage, government, and money are therefore likely to startle or offend people who hold conservative views on any of these subjects. For example, St. John Ervine, an Irish playwright and a friend of Shaw, spends a great deal of space in his biography of Shaw (*Bernard Shaw: His Life, Work and Friends*) explaining why Shaw's socialism is wrong. He is especially concerned with the sameness and regimentation that socialism might create if it were to replace the capitalist economic system. He distrusts the mass of humanity. He is least friendly to those plays which have a large political or economic factor, such as *Major Barbara* and *The Apple Cart*.

Another man who was friendly with Shaw personally but critical of his ideas was Gilbert K. Chesterton. His book, *George Bernard Shaw* (1909), was one of the earliest studies of Shaw and his work, and it is still one of the best, as a result of Chesterton's own fine mind and witty expression. The book combines affectionate appreciation of Shaw's honesty, seriousness, and independence with distress at the way Shaw rejects the usual ideas about sin and guilt; for Chesterton had a deeply religious nature himself and eventually became a Roman Catholic.

Shaw's discussions of sex have always created enemies. In the beginning of his career he was thought too outspoken: an early play, Mrs. Warren's Profession, completely broke the rules of censorship and could not be produced. Later the opposite was true. Certain writers who looked upon the sexual impulse as the basis of human behavior were shocked because Shaw felt that certain other parts of life (work, devotion to human betterment) were more important than sex. Among these writers were D. H. Lawrence and Frank Harris. They found him and his work lacking in sexuality and therefore incomplete. The American drama critic George Jean Nathan wrote an essay published in 1931 which lists all the places in his plays where the characters show a distrust or a dislike of sex. *Caesar and Cleopatra* is prominently mentioned. This essay is probably the least thoughtful expression of this idea about Shaw's writing. It is reprinted by Louis Kronenberger in *George Bernard Shaw: A Critical Survey*.

There are also segments of Shaw's thought which are regarded by almost everyone as eccentric or wrongheaded. For example, his ideas on medicine seem cranky rather than critical. He does not have very much respect for the idea of germs. He is violently opposed to vaccination against smallpox.

Then, too, some of his ideas are easy to make fun of, though on careful consideration there is nothing silly about them. Shaw was a vegetarian. When he was in his forties, his health became poor for a while, and doctors told him it was absolutely necessary to begin eating meat. Shaw refused. He could not bring himself to eat the flesh of slaughtered fellow creatures. He wrote at the time that, if he did die, his funeral procession would consist of oxen, sheep, poultry, and even fish, all mourning the man who would rather die than eat them.

The gentle humor of the passage is touching. Looking back, one must respect the personal habits of a man who lived to be ninety-four years old. But it was easy for a critic who wanted to get an easy laugh in Shaw's lifetime to say that his plays would improve if he ate steak, as the American critic Huneker did.

We may say, then, that comments on Bernard Shaw as a thinker range from the thoughtfully critical to the crudely hostile. But there are also writers who give a more balanced view of Shaw's ideas. A careful explanation may be found in Eric Bentley's *Bernard Shaw*.

Shaw The Playwright

Discussion of Shaw as playwright usually concerns his character portrayals. Most commentators agree on the liveliness and wit of the plays, but they argue about whether the characters themselves are convincing human beings. Some critics claim that the characters do not have the complexity and warmth of real people. They are only types, or representations of ideas, rather than human beings. Archibald Henderson, the author of the most important biography of Shaw, believes this. He calls Shaw's characters, "intellectual abstractions." Other critics feel that, while Shaw's characters are not absolutely realistic, Shaw is able to create a convincing manner of thought and speech for each of them. St. John Ervine says of Shaw's dialogue that it has "the rich tone of an unusual mind and yet is faithful to the nature of the people who speak it."

Homer E. Woodbridge, in *George Bernard Shaw, Creative Artist,* writes of the immense vividness of Shaw's portraits. He says that in Shaw's plays there is a group of unforgettable people who have become a living part of our literary heritage.

Some critics have also discussed the structure of Shaw's plays. Shaw himself pointed out in the preface to *Caesar and Cleopatra* that there is nothing new about the structure of his plays. He tells old stories in familiar ways. Only his ideas make his plays new.

Most critics agree with Shaw's own estimate. But to this they add the comment that even if Shaw's plays are not revolutionary, they are very competently put together. By this they mean that the plays tend to have a beginning, a middle, and an end, and that they move along at a quick pace with many interesting changes of mood and feeling. Only in his last plays did Shaw let his interest in ideas make his plays slow-moving and somewhat disorganized.

A useful study of Shaw with emphasis on dramatic structure is C. B. Purdom's *A Guide to the Plays of Bernard Shaw.* Purdom analyzes the fine points of structure in the plays. He stresses the importance of the comic protagonist-the main character who understands the significance of what is happening. Caesar is the **protagonist** in *Caesar and Cleopatra.*

Shaw's Style

Critical comment on Shaw's writing style is overwhelmingly favorable. A few people do object to the sledgehammer forcefulness with which Shaw pounds home his ideas. One critic says that there are no lyrical (poetic) passages in Shaw's plays. (Caesar's speech to the Sphinx seems to contradict this statement.) But almost every serious critic in his own way expresses admiration for Shaw's prose, which sounds simple, but which actually is a triumph of economy, clarity, and strength.

Eric Bentley remarks that to understand how much more than "simple" Shaw's writing is, you need only see an ordinary Hollywood movie and a movie of a Shaw play in the same day. The flabbiness and flatness of the first give a clue to the control and force of the second. The modern poet W. H. Auden compares Shaw's writing to the music of Rossini, the great Italian composer of comic opera who wrote *The Barber of Seville*. Shaw has, he says, the same tunefulness, humor, vivacity, and clarity in his words as the master composer has in his music.

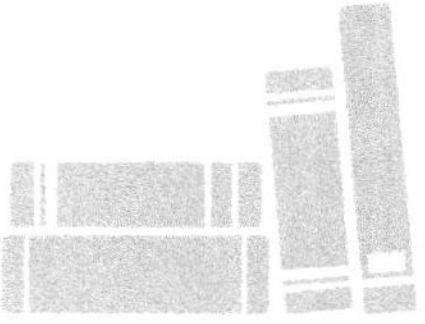

GEORGE BERNARD SHAW

MAN AND SUPERMAN

INTRODUCTION: A COMEDY AND A PHILOSOPHY (1901-1903)

Note

In making a table of characters, it is useful to adhere to the distinction Shaw provides in his title. Most of the play is the Comedy. But in Act III, the major characters of the Comedy participate in a dream sequence and become the characters of the Philosophy.

THE CHARACTERS OF THE COMEDY (ACTS I AND II; PARTS 1 AND 3 OF ACT III, AND ACT IV)

John Tanner

The hero; an imposing, bearded man of near middle age; a fluent talker; calls himself a Member of the Idle Rich Class, as well as a Revolutionist.

Ann Whitefield

A beautiful, intelligent, instinctively feminine young woman.

Roebuck Ramsden

A man past sixty, self-important, proper.

Octavius Robinson

An undistinguished young man, a poet and worshipper of Ann.

Violet Robinson

His sister, self-possessed, direct, business-like.

Hector Malone

A young American secretly married to Violet.

Mr. Malone

Hector's father, a very rich man.

Henry Straker

Tanner's capable chauffeur.

Mendoza

The leader of a band of brigands in the Sierra Nevadas of Spain.

Mrs. Whitefield

Ann's mother.

Miss Ramsden

Roebuck's spinster sister. Parlormaid, Spanish Officers, Mendoza's Men.

THE CHARACTERS OF THE PHILOSOPHY (ACT III; PART 2)

Don Juan

The hero of legend and of Mozart's opera *Don Giovanni*; John Tanner in another guise.

Ana

Donna Ana of Mozart's opera and much like Ann Whitefield.

The Devil

Mendoza added to Satan.

The Statue

The Commander in the opera, Ramsden in the Comedy.

PREFACE

Also known as the Epistle Dedicatory, or explanatory letter, to A. B. Walkley, a dramatic critic and friend of Shaw. Since it is supposed to be letter, Shaw does not provide headings for this preface. Its divisions prove to be approximately as follows:

(1) An introductory section. Shaw reminds Walkley that 15 years ago the two of them used the columns of theatre and music criticism at their disposal as vehicles of propaganda for their views of life and society. Walkley at some time asked Shaw why he did not write a play on the legend of Don Juan, and now Shaw says that he has and is presenting it along with this letter. He goes on to compare his temperament with that of Walkley and finds himself always the preacher, the man of conscience who is bothered by seeing people complacent and comfortable when they ought to be uncomfortable with the conditions of social existence they find around them.

(2) The treatment of sexual attraction in contemporary English drama. Shaw reminds Walkley of his, Shaw's long-standing objections to the way the subject of sex is treated in English plays of the time. Most of them show men and women in love, yet do not allow their characters to discuss their natural, mutual attraction, which is never made "the mainspring of the action." Those plays attempting to treat the sex question, Shaw says, are shallow and evasive because they concentrate on secondary issues instead of on the main issue of the frank relations of men and women openly discussed. So he has

tried to write a different kind of play upon the **theme** of man and woman and an unusual kind of play about Don Juan, the legendary figure of the lover.

(3) The history of Don Juan in literature. Shaw knows Walkley will not be interested in the popular image of Don Juan, the libertine lover, but in Don Juan taken "in the philosophic sense." The original Don Juan, a young Spanish nobleman, can distinguish good and evil, but by following his own instincts, he is brought into conflict with law and social institutions, which forces him to defend himself by any means. This Don, invented by a sixteenth-century Spanish monk, is the enemy of God and too clever for human antagonists. Finally, he is cast into hell by supernatural agency. The monk's tale urges the reader to repent and reform his ways before it is too late. But, as Shaw points out, the world learned a different lesson from the one intended and men become attracted to a hero who was the devil's disciple and defied God. Thereafter, the Don met varying fortunes in literary, dramatic, and musical treatment. And now, at the beginning of the twentieth century, his story is out of date and after Mozart's opera, hard to improve upon. So what is left for Shaw to do? What parts of the Don's Story are usable in a modern *Don Juan* play?

(4) Don Juan in the twentieth century. Since the first Don's time our notions of hell and repentance have changed radically. Too, society now is in the control not of the nobility but of the middle class, whose opinion is felt everywhere. Women are no longer as vulnerable as the women of Mozart's opera and have the support of law and society in the event of any wrong done them. In fact, women now (and probably always) are superior to men in the battle of the sexes. Man has been tamed and become thoughtful, conscientious, philosophic, concerned more with prolonging the race and less with gratifying his pleasures. Thus, Don Juan today is not like his old self and as the modern hero of

Man and Superman (John Tanner), unlike Mozart's Don. To find his ancestor, the reader will have to look in Act III of the play, where the Don of the opera holds a philosophic dialogue with other figures from Mozart, the lady, the statue, and the Devil.

(5) The aims of men today: nourishment and children. The ambition of the ordinary man today is to gain the means of keeping himself as a gentleman, and he expends his time and energy in pursuing riches at any cost (nourishment). The ambition of most women is to get married and bear children. In this men and women are following the dictates of Nature, broadly speaking, but they do it unscientifically, with no concern for the health of society or the consequences of bad social and political planning. The modern Englishman may be vital enough, but he runs the danger of someday being outclassed by beings superior in imagination.

(6) The conceptions of the *Don Juan* play as Shaw has written it. The subject of *Man and Superman* is not nourishment, but sexual attraction. The pretense that man pursues women is exposed, as it is in many of Shakespeare's comedies, where the heroine goes after her man and gets him. So here - Don Juan is the object of a "tragi-comic love chase," who protests to the end that he will not be captured by the woman who is in need of him to help her with Nature's urgent work of reproduction. Male vanity and hypocrisy disparage the woman for taking the initiative in this matter, instead of waiting in maidenly modesty to be wooed; but women have the pain of childbearing and men the advantages of their service. Shaw compares woman to a spider waiting motionless for a fly (her man). If it threatens to get away from her, she sets out actively to capture it.

(7) Genius and sex. The men of genius who produce impressive works of art are intellectually conscious of Nature's

purpose and are like women in their dedication to what is vital to them (their art). They are filled with a "philosophic consciousness of Life" that struggles to assert itself in their works, and they are free from excessive rule by sex. But their works usually give only fantastic notions of sex and are filled with special pleading.

(8) Politics and sex. It becomes increasingly urgent that a nation's citizens be bred to a capacity for governing the country wisely and well. To effect this, there must be a biological strengthening of the electorate, democratic education and progress having failed to bring about a genuinely intelligent citizenry. Some of these matters are touched upon in the handbook John Tanner is supposed to have written and that can be found following the text of the play (see below, *The Revolutionist's Handbook*).

(9) The literary influences upon *Man And Superman*. Shaw knows the difficulties of producing not only such a long play as *Man and Superman* but also such an intellectually challenging one. But it is meant for an audience of philosophers, which he has always wanted. Shaw owes his inspiration for some of the characters to several sources: For example, Straker to H. G. Wells, and Ann to the medieval play Everyman (she is Everywoman; that is, representative of all womankind).

(10) The artist-philosophers. Who and what are they? Those artists (painters, musicians, or writers) whose work offers a vision of life that is ennobling; artists who are not "romancers" or escapists pandering to the ordinary man's appetites. Instead, they ask a man to recognize forces beyond and greater than himself, ask him to experience true joy by recognizing a purpose greater than making himself selfishly and conventionally happy, ask him to become something like "a force of Nature."

Artist-philosophers - men like John Bunyan, author of *Pilgrim's Progress*; William Blake, the eighteenth-century poet, painter, and mystic; Leo Tolstoy, the Russian novelist; Richard Wagner, the German composer; Friedrich Nietzsche, the nineteenth-century philosopher. These men do not accept the world simply as they find it. In one way or another they probe it, criticize it, and preach at it if necessary, and try to improve it. Shaw says he wants to be counted among them and refuses to be only a writer paid to amuse or an artist for art's sake alone. He has convictions that are important to him and he is struggling with resistant materials: Here he compares himself to a wire carrying electricity - to give off light and heat.

Comment

This is one of the most important of Shaw's prefaces, especially the closing sections on the artist-philosophers. Shaw tells us much about his ideals, his purpose in writing, his standards for lasting fame. His conception of the artist is lofty and demanding of himself as well as others. In the light of it he finds Shakespeare and Dickens more artists than philosophers because they did not co-ordinate their representations of life in any systematic way. This is an unorthodox opinion and earned Shaw adverse criticism, just as his remarks on sexual attraction unsettled many readers.

ACT ONE

Setting

Roebuck Ramsden's study, London, 1901. Roebuck Ramsden, a man of means and of what he considers advanced views, is studying the morning's mail when the parlor maid announces Octavius Robinson, who appears dressed in black and grieving over the death of his benefactor, Mr. Whitefield. Ramsden offers him consolation, saying that he knows Mr. Whitefield always hoped that someday Octavius would marry his daughter Ann. This thought cheers Octavius and then makes him despair because he is not ambitious enough for her. As far as he can see, says Ramsden, Octavius has only one drawback - his friendship with John Tanner, a copy of whose outrageous *Revolutionist's Handbook and Pocket Companion* Ramsden takes up from his desk. Although all the young people may have been childhood companions, Octavius must take an adult stand now and forbid Ann any intimacy with Tanner. The man's professions of Anarchism and Free Love cannot be tolerated, and Octavius knows what a liberal he, Ramsden, has always been! The maid re-enters to say that John Tanner is upstairs with Miss Ramsden and has come with Mrs. Whitefield, Ann, and Violet Robinson.

Now Tanner bursts into the room, holding a copy of Mr. Whitefield's will, which he thrusts at Ramsden along with the news that the two of them have been appointed guardians of Ann and her sister Rhoda (who does not appear in the play). Tanner wants to refuse guardianship because, he argues, Ann will do anything she likes and then attribute it to the wish of her guardians; and Ramsden wants to refuse holding anything jointly with Tanner. Really, says Tanner, Octavius must marry Ann and get her off his hands, though, as Tanner has often pointed out, Octavius will not have, as he naively believes, a lifetime of happiness with her but rather a hell on earth. Increasingly annoyed by Tanner's words and behavior, Ramsden takes *The Revolutionist's Handbook* and throws it into the wastebasket. Octavius is sent to get Ann, leaving Tanner and Ramsden to discuss their irreconcilable differences. Tanner says he is proud of what Ramsden calls his impudence and thinks Ramsden with his respectability forty years behind the times. Octavius returns with Ann and her mother. Ramsden explains the dilemma facing them and asks Ann to choose between him and Tanner for guardian. But Ann insists upon respecting what she calls her father's sacred wishes and it is only after some discussion that the original joint guardianship is accepted, just as Ann wants. She has a habit of nicknaming everybody - Ramsden is Granny, Tanner is Jack, and Octavius is Ricky-ticky-tavy; and after charming the men into accepting her pet names for them, she leaves the room, followed by her mother and Ramsden. Now Tanner turns to Octavius and warns him that Ann will swallow him alive if he marries her. Over Octavius' protests Tanner explains his view of woman. Man is an instrument of her purpose, and though she may appear self-sacrificing and unselfish in little things, she is secretly working for Nature's blind purpose of vital creation. She enslaves man, and to Octavius' reply that it makes no difference as long as a man is happy in his slavery, Tanner reminds him that Octavius pretends to be a poet, an artist dedicated to art. The mother-woman, he warns, will engage the artist in a struggle and will try to use him up, to destroy his capacity to enlighten mankind through his creations by converting that capacity to her own uses.

They are interrupted by the return of Ann and Ramsden with fresh news. They have just learned from her that Octavius' sister Violet is pregnant though unmarried. Shocked, Octavius wants to know who is the man responsible, while Tanner praises Violet for fulfilling her highest role as a mother-woman. He sends Octavius to bring her down, reminding him that Violet is going to risk her life in childbearing. Ramsden leaves to go upstairs too and Ann remains behind with Tanner. In the long scene between them that follows, Jack tells Ann he thinks her a hypocrite without conscience, but fascinating. They then review their relations with each other and with Octavius, whom Ann tempted even as a child. She had a way, Jack remembers, of drawing out a boy's secrets and weaknesses without revealing any of her own. But he had a secret he never told her. It was about the birth in him of a sense of principle, of study and obligation, of a soul and of "moral passion," the only genuine passion. There are other passions, says Ann. None stronger than the moral, replies Jack; it makes him a reformer, a shatterer of empty creeds and false idols, makes him seem destructive when he intends to be ultimately constructive. He says he loves creation, even in a woman and in Ann. It was her creative instinct that led her to tie him to her. But their childhood compact ended as he became aware of himself as a new person, and he vowed he would never let a woman enslave him and so put him off doing the world's necessary, important work out of sentimental consideration for her (woman is well able to take care of herself!). He compares Ann (as he has done already before Octavius) to a boa constrictor winding itself about its prey, which makes Ann laugh and throw her feather boa about his neck, then her arms. Jack says Octavius will never escape her because she wants him. But Ann warns Jack not to be too clever, he may not know as much about her as he thinks. He admits he does not feel entirely safe with her, that she exerts a subtle spell, and he moves to signal the others by bell to come back.

Ramsden returns with Octavius and with Miss Ramsden, who announces impatiently that Violet will not confide in her friends and insists upon being near the man who has ruined her. The parlor maid comes in to report the arrival of a cab Violet has ordered to take her away. Violet herself then enters, ashamed of nothing and angry with her supposed friends, even with Tanner who congratulates her on her courage. When she realizes he is approving her unmarried state, she addresses him and the others sharply, telling them she is secretly married and they had no right to suppose her a fallen woman. It is her husband's wish that she not reveal his name. Now no one's apologies satisfy her and she leaves the room abruptly, while Tanner points out that they all must bow to the institution of marriage.

Comment

This first act shows *Man and Superman* to be a modern comedy of manners and ideas, and the reader should not overlook the comedy out of preoccupation with the ideas. The comedy lies, for example, in surprise. Note the way we are led to expect that Violet is a disgraced woman, to accept Tanner's broadminded sympathy for her, and then are told she is married after all and resents misplaced concern. The joke is partly on us but also on Tanner, who always supports the unpopular cause. It is a joke about his character, and comedy of character richly abounds in Shaw's plays. Note the repeated humor of Ann's pretending to give in to the wishes of others, while all the time she knows exactly what she wants to do, just as Tanner says she does. Note how the dialogue aids the development of Shaw's characterization, how Tarner's impertinents, cutting remarks puncture the high-sounding, even pompous, bluster of Ramsden. The very rhythms of Tanner's speeches are quick and pointed whereas Ramsden's sentences and whole cast of mind seem slow, deliberate and old-fashioned. As for ideas, Tanner's account of the growth in him of moral passion should be kept in mind. Moral passion is a distinguishing mark of a major Shaw hero. Caesar (*Caesar and Cleopatra*) possesses it, as does Undershaft (*Major Barbara*) and Joan (*Saint Joan*). Tanner's description of the relation of the sexes is important too in light of the remarks in the Preface about the Don Juan hero. Note Ann's response. She playfully throws her boa around Jack (is she like the constrictor?), and we wonder indeed if Tavy is the man she wants. Shaw may be employing the device of **foreshadowing** here, giving us a hint of what is to come.

ACT TWO

Setting

Outside Mrs. Whitefield's house near London.

The curtain rises on Tanner and his chauffeur, Henry Straker, who has just succeeded in fixing Tanner's touring car, which has broken down on the drive (the directions call for the car on stage). A motoring party has been arranged: Tanner is to take Ann's sister with him, while the American, Hector Malone, is to take Ann, Octavius, and Mrs. Whitefield in his new steam car. Octavius comes from the house now and is introduced to Straker, whom Tanner praises as a model of efficiency, the New Man with no use for the aristocracy and a strong pride in his own class. Straker goes off and Octavius tells Tanner that he was brute enough to offend Ann by proposing to her last night. Tanner repeats his warnings that Ann is not being pursued by Tavy but is herself doing the chasing and, like the bee in the natural-history lesson, has marked Tavy for her prey. But Tavy puts Jack's remarks down to cynicism and says he is too much in love to pay them any attention. Straker returns with a newspaper report of an automobile speed record that he thinks he can beat. This reminds Tavy to give Tanner a note from Rhoda saying that Ann has forbidden her to go on a drive with Jack, which can only mean that his opinions are too dangerous for a girl. Straker leaves as Ann enters from the house. She asks Tavy to go in and amuse Hector Malone and she stays behind with Tanner. He accuses her of having poisoned her sister's mind against him, to which Ann replies that she did so, if he wants to call it that, out of respect for her mother's fear of Jack. This provokes him to an attack on mothers who dominate their daughters and impose upon them their own timidity and fear of a rival in the male. A daughter, says Jack, must emancipate herself from her mother if she is to call her soul her own and he now urges Ann to do so. Carried away by his eloquence he invites her to join him in a fast motor trip to France and across the desert to North Africa. To his surprise she takes him seriously and accepts, arguing that no one could say a word against her traveling with her guardian.

Jack starts to protest, but he is interrupted by the arrival from the house of Mrs. Whitefield, Hector, Ramsden, and Octavius. Ann tells her mother she is going with Jack to Nice. Hector is introduced to Tanner, and he proposes joining the party, taking along Miss Robinson. Ann and her mother withdraw while the men try to explain to Hector the impossibility of taking Violet, a married woman whose husband no one knows. Now Violet is seen approaching from the house, and Hector asks the other men to leave him to speak a few words to her. When they find they are alone, Hector and Violet embrace, and we learn that he is the mysterious husband. She has made him promise not to reveal their marriage owing to his father's objections: The senior Mr. Malone wants his son to marry an English noblewoman, though he himself is a manufacturer of office furniture. The young couple try to think of a way to take Violet on the trip and leave to look over Hector's new car as Straker and Tanner return. Tanner asks his chauffeur to arrange things so as to leave Octavius and Ann together as much as possible. Straker is amused by this and hums a melody, as he does when he cannot speak what he thinks. Tanner asks for an explanation - and gets it. It is not Tavy Ann is interested in capturing - it is Tanner she wants! It is all clear to Jack now, he is the prey. He makes a quick decision. He and Straker will leave at once, and 'Enry will have his chance to break that speed record by driving south as fast as he can, from where they can sail to some country where men are protected from women. Tanner hurriedly starts up the motor, and Straker has to run after him to catch up as the car plunges forward.

Comment

Another piece of comic plotting is notable in this act. With Hector and Violet we are reminded of the **conventions** of ancient farce by which lovers may be secretly engaged or married. Here the **convention** is used not only to surprise and amuse us but to make a comment on the snobbishness of the English and American middle classes. Hector's father is a businessman, but he would have a title in his family and so force his son to desperate measures. The sudden disclosure by Straker that Ann is pursuing Tanner is a cleverly managed **climax** to this act. The relations of Ann and Jack are both comic and serious (as is the play). These two remind one of another pair of lovers in old plays. They are much like the lovers in some Shakespeare's comedies (compare Beatrice and Benedick in *Much Ado about Nothing*) who treat each other to sarcasm and a show of hostility or indifference when all along they are in love and will declare themselves only at the end of the play. Here Shaw is varying that conception somewhat. Tanner is not romantically in love with Ann, but he admits he finds her fascinating. As for Ann, she does not try to match his wit; she waits coolly, letting him talk on, marking him for her own.

ACT THREE, PART ONE

Setting

Evening in the Sierra Nevadas of Spain. Outside a cave in the mountains, Mendoza, the chief of a band of brigands, is addressing his men. They are a mixed lot of Europeans, dressed inappropriately in odd-looking city clothing, independently minded tramps who have fled the social system that condemns men to drudgery and a life starved of beauty.

Mendoza is trying to moderate a discussion of what social order is best for men, but all the gang want to talk at once. He reminds them that they are here in the mountains not to discuss abstruse questions but to hold up motor cars from the luxury resorts, rob their owners, and redistribute their wealth among the working classes. A watchman rushes in to announce the approach of a car. A moment later Tanner and Straker are led in under guard. Mendoza introduces himself as a man who lives by robbing the rich; Tanner presents himself as one who lives by robbing the poor; and so an air of good humor is established. Mendoza invites his captives to sit by the fire and dismisses his men. He wants to settle the matter of ransom, which leads to talk about the existing social order. Mendoza tells them about himself. He and his gang were not suited to middle-class society and so turned to brigandage. He was once a waiter, he reveals, in love with an enchanting girl who scorned him. He longs, he says, to be an Englishman, and for the girl he loves, Louisa. When he hears this name and the description of the girl, Straker starts up. It turns out that Mendoza has been talking about his sister, and 'Enry wants to challenge the chief until Tanner comes between them. Mendoza now wants to show some poems he has written about Louisa, but Tanner stops him, saying it is unworthy of him to ruin himself for a woman like any romantic hack poet, and especially here in this exhilarating atmosphere. Mendoza reads aloud anyway. Tanner and Straker doze off by the fire, and in a moment Mendoza lies down to sleep himself.

Comment

After this scene the Comedy will be interrupted. Note the character of Mendoza. An outcast of society and a fearless leader of brigands, he is easily undone by a woman. He is somewhat like Octavius, only harder of intellect. The speech and dress of his gang are comically at odds with their romantic environment.

ACT THREE, PART TWO - THE PHILOSOPHY

Note

The scene that follows is not always staged as part of *Man and Superman*. In production it may be excerpted without hurting the continuity of the Comedy, and sometimes the Philosophy is given as an independent play. Its action as such is minimal. It is chiefly a dialogue, like one of Plato's, where the main interest is in the exchange of ideas.

As they sleep, Tanner and Mendoza dream, and what follows in a vision they have but find hard to recollect upon awakening. The landscape darkens, the fire fades, and they seem to be surrounded by a void. Music is heard, strains from Mozart's *Don Giovanni*, after which a bodiless yet visible man appears in the dress of a sixteenth-century Spanish nobleman and looking a little like Tanner - in fact, his name is Don Juan Tenorio. Gradually three other characters come on the scene, each identified by musical **themes** from the opera: an old woman, who is soon magically transformed into a young woman and becomes Donna Ana (Ann); her father, the Statue or Commander of the opera who, while defending his daughter's honor, was killed by Juan (he reminds one of Ramsden); and the Devil, derived more from Mephistopheles in Gounod's opera *Faust* than from Mozart and reminding one of Mendoza. We are to understand that these characters are conversing in Hell, the home of the Devil. Juan has been placed there in punishment for the murder of the Commander, but he is not at all happy in Hell, for him the place of what is unreal and where empty conceptions of Love and Beauty are idly worshipped. Ana is resentful of being there because she thinks herself a respectable woman who ought to be in Heaven. The Statue, on the other hand, comes from Heaven, where he has been restless, and hopes to remain in Hell, which he finds lives up to its reputation as a place where one may easily amuse and gratify oneself. The Devil tells of his dislike for Heaven, a boring place he chose to leave, a place stuffy, respectable people like to go because they think they owe it to their position. Now a discussion ensues in which many topics are raised. The main points of the dialogue carried chiefly through Juan and the Devil, are summarized here under topic headings.

Heaven versus Hell

Devil: Heaven is cold and tedious, whereas Hell is the place for the cultivation of those satisfactions to be found in the pursuit of personal happiness and in the graces of life. There love, beauty, music, art are prized, and all that is forbiddingly moral, severe, or unlovely is expelled.

Juan: Hell is the home of those who avoid the challenge of reality, who wish to escape it and live an endless romance. On Earth men are slaves to reality, which subdues them in the form of physical need and appetite. But in Heaven men master reality, preferring to face danger, hard work, and obligation to improve existence rather than living out self-deluding lies as they do in Hell, the home of idle dreamers.

Life and Death

Juan: The work of Heaven is to help Life in its struggle from simple and brutelike forms of organization to higher forms. As man ascends the ladder of evolution, Life must be helped to make his brain avoid blundering and his reason to become effectual.

Devil: Man's brain works only for evil. Man gives his best energies not to the arts of life but to the weapons of death. His imagination is inspired by death and his tolerance for poverty and pestilence demonstrates the power death has over him.

Juan: Man is essentially a coward and his civilization is founded on cowardice, which he calls respectability. It is base living that degrades man, not death. But men can be moved by a noble idea to fight for it heroically. Even a selfish man is capable of dedication to a purpose that is superior to his own interests if he convinced he is doing a piece of Heavenly work.

Man and Woman; the Life Force; Progress

Juan: Man and woman serve Nature's purpose of continuing the race of humanity. Woman is totally absorbed in this, but man, who needs more to occupy him, has gone on to make civilization. There is an impulse in him - call it the Life Force - that doggedly tries to win for man greater self-knowledge. Life has been trying to refine the power of man's brain and intellect in order to aid him to discover Life's purposes and so prevent their being thwarted by selfish stupidity or shortsightedness. The true hero is the "philosophic man," he who searches out and seeks to fulfill "the inner will of the world." Other kinds of men are to be distrusted, especially the artist, for having delivered man over to the unceasing idealization of woman, beauty, and personal satisfaction. I (Juan) have been made wiser, if not happier by Life's throwing me at last into the arms of woman. The relation between me and woman was not friendly. The sexual relation never is, because man and woman are agents of creative energy, which has no concern for man-made virtues like chastity, honorable marriage, ideal love, and the like. Eventually, man will try to breed a superhuman race and so find the purpose of Life now hidden by romantic illusion. Man must improve existence and make himself more profoundly self-aware by facing stern natural and biological necessities. The Devil's mission is to direct him into the search for unending pleasure, getting him to abandon his will and making him unhappy, bored, restless. When man strives to make meaningful the virtues he now pays lip service to, he will make progress.

Devil: Progress is an illusion, the movements of history deceptive. Man's sense of purpose is not necessarily Nature's.

Juan: The philosophic brain in the grip of the Life Force is part of Nature and gives man power to choose the path he wants to go. In Hell man drifts; in Heaven he steers the ship of his fate.

The Superman

The dialogue is about over, and Juan asks the Devil to point the way to the frontiers of Heaven, then leaves. The Devil curses him as a Life Worshipper who resists his temptations, and he criticizes the celebration of superhuman endeavor and faculties, this new cult of the Superman. As he and the Commander descend into Hell, Ana cries out to them to tell her where the Superman is to be found. He has not been created yet, replies the Devil. Then, Ana says, her work is not done, she must find a father for the man to come, the Superman. Then she too vanishes into the void, and the vision is ended.

Comment

The Dialogue in Hell (sometimes called Don Juan in Hell) concentrates a great part of Shaw's philosophy and his idealism. In every respect it is a perfect example of the style and manner to which the adjective "Shavian" applies. Consider the main paradox or reversal of accepted values on which the philosophy is constructed: Hell is not a place of vivid torment, as has been traditionally painted, but a place of eternal and undemanding pleasures for those who like them; and Heaven is not conceived of as a resting place for the virtuous but as a place for the "masters of reality." Of course, to Juan, Hell is a torment because a man drifts there and is without aim or purpose. Shaw, then, upsets our expectations of what Heaven and Hell will stand for in his play. As for the characters of the Philosophy, Shaw keeps them close to, but not always identical with, the characters of the Comedy, and reminiscent of their counterparts in *Don Giovanni* (Note how he quotes passages of music from the opera). Juan is as talkative as Tanner; the Devil is much slyer than Mendoza; Ana, like Ann, is concerned for her reputation and talks of her duty, but she is more subdued than Ann and far less clever; the Commander is altogether much more agreeable than Ramsden and admires Juan's ability to debate with the Devil. Note again how Shaw makes us see Juan in an unusual way. It is the point of the Philosophy, and of the Comedy as well, that Juan is not the libertine seducer of women that legend has made him. He is a philosophic man of moral passion who follows the promptings of the Life Force (the underlined phrases summarize the leading concepts of the play). His meeting with women brings about a conflict between the man of genius, who wants to do the work of the world, and the woman bent instinctively on the work of Nature, which means keeping him tied to her. The engagement between them is not frivolous; it is deadly serious and inspires fear and wonder in them both. Although *Man and Superman* makes comedy of the Tanner-Ann relationship, it is comedy with a purpose: It uses the formula of boy-meets-girl in a new way, reverses it or inverts it, making the girl chase the boy, and shows the meaning of that chase. It should be said too that Tanner-Juan, the philosopher-genius, recognizes the necessity of obeying Nature - even welcomes it - and feels the better man for his surrender. But - and this is a crucial point - he refuses to idealize the sexual relationship or the institutions of courtship and marriage that disguise it essential fierceness. This he leaves to the poet-dreamers like Octavius and Mendoza. To do Heaven's work and be a master of reality, the philosophic man must live without illusions (compare Caesar).

ACT THREE, PART THREE - THE COMEDY (CONTINUED)

One of the guards cries out the arrival of another automobile, which wakes Tanner, Mendoza, and Straker. Mendoza is told that soldiers are coming to capture him, but Tanner reassures him that he has no charges to bring. Now enter Ann, Violet, Hector, Ramsden, followed by Octavius. It is disclosed that Ann has urged Hector to catch up with Jack, who cries, "The Life Force! I am lost." Mendoza suddenly recognizes all of these people from his days as a waiter in a London hotel and is annoyed at not being treated courteously. A car full of soldiers stops. An officer comes forward, looks over Mendoza and his crew, then asks Tanner who they are. There is a moment of suspense - then Tanner answers that they are his escort.

Comment

As the Comedy resumes, note the significance of Tanner's "The Life Force! I am lost." It is a remnant of his dream. Mendoza's recognition of the motoring party from his hotel days is a theatrically effective stroke. But this is not a "realistic" play, as we have seen; and even if it is objected to, this piece of farcical invention does not affect the main intentions of the play.

ACT FOUR

Setting

Garden of a villa in Granada.

As the act begins, Straker is speaking with Hector Malone, Senior, an elderly American businessman who has just intercepted a note sent ambiguously to the hotel by Violet. Intended for his son, the note urges Hector to come to the villa quickly, and so Mr. Malone has arrived, puzzled and suspicious. Violet comes in to greet him, and they discuss his son's affairs. Mr. Malone warns her that he does not intend that Hector should marry anyone without a title. Violet is not easily intimidated by old Malone's threats to stop his support of Hector once he marries a middle-class girl; in fact, she begins cleverly to change his mind when Hector rushes in to accuse his father of treachery in having opened a private letter. Their quarrel is interrupted by the arrival of Tanner, Ann, Octavius, and Ramsden; but only for a moment. Hector declares he will defy his father and marry Violet, which shocks the men, who think Violet already married. The misunderstanding increases rapidly until Hector can bear it no longer and tells them all that he and Violet are husband and wife. He then refuses any of his father's money or offers of assistance by Octavius and Tanner. From now on, he says proudly, he will be a Worker. His father is immediately abject and wants to make peace. Hector is feeling too self-important now to accept money; but Violet, after sending him ahead, takes her father-in-law's money in an efficient, realistic way that makes him her grateful slave. Tanner, of course, notes this and comments on it to Ramsden, then introduces the two men. They go out together, Malone explaining the business that has brought him here, something to do with buying up shares in a firm called Mendoza, Limited. This too amuses Tanner, who tells it to Octavius, walking in the garden, and leaves.

Ann comes in on her way to the villa, and Octavius again tearfully confesses his love. She tells him it is her parents' wish that she marry Jack. She hopes Tavy will remain a bachelor for her sake; she would so like, she says as she leaves, to make him less foolish about women. But Tavy, a poet at heart, is inconsolable. He is sobbing quietly when Mrs. Whitefield comes in, on return from a shopping trip, and asks what is the matter. She explains that it is Ann's not her, wish that Ann marry Jack; but Tavy cannot bring himself to suspect Ann of deceit, and he goes out as Tanner comes back. Now Jack discusses Ann with her mother, reviewing his charges: Ann is a liar, a coquette, and conventional, and he will not accept the general presumption that he and Ann will marry. In fact, he tells Ann so when they are alone shortly. But he is drawn to her magnetically, against his will. He is in the grip of the Life Force, he says, ready to sell out his ideals and do Nature's will by becoming a husband. But he wants to know why Ann chooses him and not Octavius. She quietly explains that Octavius does not have the temperament for marriage, and Jack recognizes for the first time that the Life Force has passed Tavy by. And now Ann reveals that she has set the trap for him from the start, by influencing her father to appoint Jack her guardian. Still Tanner denies her, and she begins to relent. But the Life

Force is too strong for them. Jack confesses his love and she her fear, after which she faints. When she is brought round, she finds everyone, including Mendoza, gathered there in the garden and tells them she has promised to marry Jack. She and Jack accept congratulations, but he announces that he will tolerate no sentimental or naive tributes to their future happiness since he and Ann have renounced happiness, as the others understand it. Violet interrupts his closing speech, but Ann encourages him to go on to keep talking. "Talking!" exclaims Tanner, at which we hear "universal laughter."

Comment

The comedy of this last act is mainly of two kinds. (1) Comedy of misunderstanding: the mix-up in the letters that begins the act and Malone's ignorance of the fact that he is talking to his daughter-in-law. (2) Comedy of reversal: Malone is determined at first to cut off his son's allowance should Hector marry against his wishes. But when Hector tells the truth and then says he will become a Worker, Malone cannot do enough to make amends; and, whereas he began by quarreling with Violet, he ends by making peace with her. Hector surprises everyone by his announcement and clears up some complicated confusion. There is surprise too in the disclosure that Malone is doing business with Mendoza's syndicate. This is not fully explained and serves as a very minor **theme**. Shaw means by their association that a capitalist is doing with a chief of brigands and that all capitalists are brigands at heart and some, like Mendoza, romantic ones. Call it surprise or reversal, the most important about-face is saved for the last pages of the act. That is Jack's assent to the Life Force after three and one-half acts of protest. His wooing of Ann is comic and yet painful for each of them. At the same time, Shaw makes comedy out of Ann's fainting and her being revived to receive the innocent and ordinary congratulations of the other main characters. There is a surprise for the audience in Ann's confession that she made a trap for Jack out of her father's will. No wonder, then, at the end Tanner can only exclaim his own futility. He talks on and on, but what good does it do? His speeches are greeted by universal laughter, which may mean not just the laughter of the other characters but the laughter of some unseen spirit somewhere in the universe.

Note, the play is followed by the text of John Tanner's *The Revolutionist's Handbook and Pocket Companion*, spoken of in the first and last act. It consists of short essays and maxims on such topics as Progress, Revolution, the Superman, Civilization, History, and it reads much like the preface.

ANALYSIS OF SELECTED CHARACTERS

John Tanner

As a member of the Idle Rich Class, and like most of the characters, he does not work for a living. He writes books on the social order. He is what used to be called a parlor pink, a Left Wing or radical aristocrat. His program of revolution is founded on philosophical premises and is designed to puncture the complacency of the middle and upper classes. He thinks acutely, talks well, and much of what he says is meant to sound sensible. At the same time we are amused by Tanner, in somewhat the way Ann is, because we know - and he knows it too - that his talking will change nothing, and he will give himself up to Ann even as he is talking against surrender. He both welcomes and fears the Life Force, is moved by the sexual relationship, and is compelled by the forms of marriage and conventional family life. Tanner is a "genius" character, with vision that sees far beyond the ordinary man's. He is a man passionately committed to making the world ready for the Superman. Indeed, Tanner is often taken for a portrait of Shaw: large, bearded, and "possibly a little mad" (see stage directions to Act One).

Ann Whitefield

Tanner says harsh things about her, though he says them wittily: She is shrewd, conniving, flirtatious, conventional, hypocritical - and totally fascinating. We see how devious her conduct can be, notably in the pretense of her duty to elders, a mask for her independent actions. And we see a kind of playful cruelty in her toying with Octavius. But she too is in the service of the Life Force, though she does not recognize it consciously as Tanner does. She has little use for ideas. Ultimately she fears the pain of creation that marriage must bring after the submission of the artist-man to the mother-woman. Her pursuit of Tanner for a husband is made by him to seem predatory (he compares her behavior to that of animals) and yet necessary. As Donna Ana, she is all respectability and outraged virtue. But at the end of the Philosophy she too awaits the Superman.

Octavius

He and Mendoza represent romantic men, poets at heart, dedicated to enshrining women, an Ann or a Louisa Straker. Octavius is almost totally ineffectual, and Ann is clever enough to see that he will remain a bachelor, the Life Force having passed him by. (Note: Tanner does not have all the insights.) He poetizes, he sobs, he is completely the victim of the strong-minded persons, who treat him with affection and some condescension.

Violet

Like Ann, though not so magnetic, she is realistic and hard as nails. She understands the privileges of her sex and her class and the ways of the world in which she moves. She does not try to change anything, only to utilize the materials at hand. Thus by simply being herself, she outwits or wins over her elders and superiors. She is a lesser version of Woman, but Woman all the same.

The Malones

They represent a contrast. Young Hector is a product of good eastern American schools and speaks with the acquired accent of class. Old Malone is a self-made man and, comically enough, a snob. An Irish immigrant and the grandson of peasants, he has made enough money to buy a title for his family if he can find one for sale. Violet out-maneuvers his objections to her very quickly and takes the money the proud Hector will not. She knows, as old Malone does, that Hector will never be much of a worker. And she is not prepared to live as the wife of a poor man.

MAJOR BARBARA (1905)

CHARACTERS

BARBARA	Daughter of Andrew Undershaft and Lady Britomart; called "major" because she holds that rank in the Salvation Army.
ANDREW UNDERSHAFT	A middle-aged munitions maker and financial power.
LADY BRITOMART	His wife, a matronly lady.
STEPHEN UNDERSHAFT	The son of the family, twenty-five.
SARAH	Another daughter.
ADOLPHUS CUSINS	A professor of Greek, in love with Barbara.
CHARLES LOMAX	A young man who wants to marry Sarah.
MORRISON	The Undershaft butler.
SNOBBY PRICE	A workman at the Salvation Army shelter in West Ham.
RUMMY MITCHENS	An old lady at the shelter.
JENNY HILL	Eighteen, an enthusiastic Salvationist.
PETER SHIRLEY	An old man at the shelter.
BILL WALKER	A young tough.
MRS. BAINES	A Commissioner in the Salvation Army.
BILTON	Foreman at Undershaft's ammunition works.

PREFACE

In the opening pages of the preface, Shaw takes to task those critics who have charged that he owes all of his originality to his reading in foreign authors, the playwright Ibsen or the philosophers Schopenhauer and Nietzsche. He maintains that he first found many of his ideas in native work and that it is unnecessary to suppose England an intellectual void. He is, he says, not alone in the treatment of some of his favorite themes: The conflict between actuality and romantic imaginings about life; the woman as being more than a passive doll and the toy of men; the superman as the savior of society.

From there on the preface deals more directly with the themes of *Major Barbara* and some of its characters. First, there is a section on the topic of *poverty,* which is the subject of the play. For Shaw poverty was the greatest of evils and the worst of crimes, and its manifestations, (lawlessness and disease, for example) are a menace to *all* of society, not only to the poor. This is the view he attributes to his hero, Andrew Undershaft, who is clear-sighted and unsentimental in his denunciation of poverty. Undershaft understands the hypocrisy of middle-class society in its thinking about the matter. The poor themselves do not want uplift or moral improvement, they want more money. And money is a desirable commodity not to be scorned or piously depreciated, for it makes life bearable and is a curse only under social conditions that are themselves a curse. Every man should have the right to money on reasonable terms, with the work that goes to earning it equitably distributed. Undershaft appreciates the truth of this position and is mystic imbued with the Life Force (see above, *Man and Superman),* an instrument of a purpose larger than himself.

Shaw defends his play from the criticism that it is an attack on and a mockery of the Salvation Army. Even the Army, he points out, does not believe that. The Army is not inconsistent either in taking money tainted by the occupation from which it derives. It is not sentimental and unrealistic. It knows that all money will be tainted until we have acquired a social organization that does not exploit the unfortunate, make profit from human weakness, or encourage the unscrupulous. Major Barbara comes to understand that poverty is not blessed. The Army itself is conducting a worthy fight, but it has its weaknesses. Among them Shaw scorns its other-worldliness, its belief that salvation is not to be achieved in this world but only in the next; its encouraging the bad habit of public confession, which deludes the sinner into thinking he can atone simply by describing his sin and his conversion. Shaw is opposed to any system of official absolution. In the play, Barbara will have nothing to do with our public Christian morality of punishment of wrong-doers, because it inspires only revenge and no fundamental change in the sinner. That morality of vindictiveness, public or private, is "Crosstianity," Shaw says — retaliation disguised as religious principle. For people to be made better, there must be a reorganization of society so that the circumstances of life can be made tolerable to people now reduced by them to crime, poverty, or depravity, and in which there will no longer be the official conspiracy of Church and State to keep things as they are. The popular Christianity of vengenace and punishment by police must be replaced by the true Christianity of equality and fellow-feeling. Otherwise the man of conscience will have to go on protesting injustice, social disorder, waste, and be thought a harmful revolutionary like the anarchist, the man driven by oppression to destroy the social order with bombs.

Two social abuses especially must be set right. (1) Every ablebodied man must work for a living, earning his wealth in proportion to his effort. (2) The systems of imprisonment and official punishment must be abolished. They only torment the prisoner and use up manpower in policing him. Worst of all, they fail to teach the great lesson that must be taught: A man's "deeds are irrevocable," the actions he takes to harm another cannot be recalled, and the value of his life is in his usefulness to society. Evil must be faced squarely so that it may be combated, true mischief recognized and not allowed to be atoned for or redeemed by punishment, pardon, or expressions of repentance.

Comment

This preface (and play) is crucial to an understanding of Shaw on the vital subject of poverty. In it he is disputing a popular notion of his time, that there must always be poor people in a world that cannot provide equally for everyone. As a Socialist, Shaw thinks poverty avoidable. Note, he calls it "a crime" and refuses to condone it or to believe in the effectiveness of supporting people in their poverty by organized charity or Christian consolation. Poverty can be eradicated by improved social organization. This preface is astute in its arguments and very helpful to an understanding of the play (see below).

ACT ONE

Setting

The library of Lady Britomart's house. January of 1906, after dinner.

Lady Britomart, troubled by family affairs, is confiding for the first time in her son Stephen. She has taken action to settle them and asks his approval. Money must be found for daughter Sarah, because her fiance, Charles Lomax, will never be able to provide adequately for them; there is the problem of older sister Barbara, who has forsaken social success for a career in the Salvation Army and who has lately acquired an admirer, Adolphus Cusins, a professor of Greek; and there is Stephen himself, for whom Lady Britomart must find a suitable match. Money must be obtained for all of them.

The conversation turns to the father of this family, Andrew Undershaft, of Lazarus and Undershaft, notorious munitions makers who virtually control Europe. Undershaft, Lady Britomart complains, has always been above the law and has arranged things in his own eccentric way. He once confessed to his wife that he was himself illegitimately born, a foundling, and now wants only another foundling, instead of his natural son, to succeed him in business, a family tradition. This has led Lady Britomart to separate from him and maintain her children independently, as well as to protect them from Undershaft's outrageous and unconventional opinions. Even so, they are all largely dependent on him for support. Accordingly, Lady Britomart now reveals, she has asked Undershaft to come in tonight to meet his daughters and fianceès and to discuss their affairs. Sarah, Barbara, Lomax, and Cusins enter now, Barbara in the uniform of a major in the Salvation Army. Lady Britomart's announcement that Undershaft is coming causes excitement. Sarah is a little alarmed, but Barbara sees his coming as an opportunity to save his soul. Lady Brit (she is so called by Cusins) cautions the children to be on their best behavior since their father has not seen them since their infancy and they must now do her credit for their upbringing.

Morrison the butler announces Undershaft, who greets his wife courteously and initially mistakes Lomax for one of his children, and makes things worse by almost instinctively passing by Stephen and acknowledging Cusins as his son. Cusins sets him straight and introduces everyone correctly. After an uncomfortable pause, the convention begins. Undershaft shows an interest in Barbara's work with the Army, which seems to create a bond between them. He says the motto of the Army : and the munitioner is the same: Blood and Fire, though the blood of the munitioner cleanses and its fire purifies. Undershaft makes no apology for his profession, arguing that he does not separate his morals and his business, that he is interested in improving the weapons of destruction and does not lend his profits to conscience-saving institutions like hospitals and cathedrals. In the discussion that follows of true morality and good men, Barbara maintains that in her experience there are no good men or scoundrels, only children of one Father, with salvation for all sinners, despite social rank or profession. Undershaft challenges her to a bargain: He will come to see her tomorrow in the Salvation shelter and let her try to save him if the next day she will visit his munitions factory. She agrees, though Undershaft warns her that she may be the one to be converted to his way of thinking, not he to hers.

At Lady Brit's suggestion that Undershaft stay for family prayers, they begin to retire to the drawing room for the service he proposes, with Barbara conducting it and Lomax on the concertina. As they go out, Lady Brit tells Cusins she knows that he has joined the Army chiefly to be near Barbara, and he in turn playfully asks her not to give him away. Left with Stephen, Lady Brit cannot resist a few tears, for she sees how powerfully the children are attracted by their father and cannot believe they will attend to her any longer.

Comment

This first act neatly establishes some of the main issues of the play and the opposed points of view, yet so effortlessly that one is tempted to overlook the skill of it. Note how Shaw makes comedy out of the tension between Lady Brit's view of things and Undershaft's. In the opening scene with Stephen we sense her exasperation with a husband who by his unconventional views has left her to cope all these years with difficult situations. Her sarcasm extends itself to Lomax, who is something of a noodle, a fashionable but not very bright young man. She is a proper matron, not unsympathetic, and puts a good face on unusual circumstances. One can see too how concerned she is that the children not find Undershaft too attractive, for she admits his power, even over herself. Barbara says very little in this act, but the challenge is laid down, the lines of conflict drawn between her and Undershaft, who interest each other. She naively wants to save his soul, does not understand that he thinks himself saved already, and mistakes his interest in the Army for a conventionally pious one. But Undershaft appears to see something likeable in her. In Cusins too, whom he mistakes for his son, thus foreshadowing the resolution of the play and providing an apt piece of symbolism (notice how much discussion there is in the play of fathers, sons, foundlings, orphans). Cusins is quick of intelligence and immediately responds to Undershaft. In short, Shaw accomplishes much in this act.

ACT TWO

Setting

The Salvation Army shelter in a poor district of London. A January morning.

In the shelter at West Ham, Snobby Price, an unemployed young painter with Socialist leanings, is complaining of his lot to Rummy Michens, a middle-aged woman who confesses to him that she pretends to be worse than she is so as to give satisfaction to the Army girl who works so hard to save her. Snobby admits he plays the same game when he makes up stories of abusing his old mother. Jenny Hill, an Army lass, comes in with Peter Shirley, a worn-out, half-starved workman, old before his time and bitterly lamenting the loss of his job in favor of a younger man. A moment later Bill appears at the door of the shelter. He is a young tough, looking for his girl, whom he accuses the Army of having warned against him. He roughs up Jenny Hill as being the one responsible, slaps Rummy when she interferes, threatens the cowardly Snobby with a beating, and is challenged by Shirley, who dares him to box with the well-known wrestler Todger Fairmile. Now Major Barbara comes in to check on the new arrivals. Shirley gives her his name and trade. Walker refuses his. Barbara then recognizes him: He is the man Jenny Hill is inside praying for. Walker tells her he came to fetch his girl. But she has gone to another shelter, Barbara informs him, has been saved and joined the Army; and she has a new boy friend in a reformed wrestler, Sergeant Todger Fairmile. Walker is baffled and angry, but Jenny comes back now to forgive him and bless him. Undershaft appears, as Barbara appeals to Walker to give over his stubbornness, his soul-tormenting pride in having hurt Jenny, and allow himself to be saved. He is about to give in when Cusins enters the Shelter yard, beating a drum, and breaks the spell of Barbara's entreaty. Swearing to get even with his girl and Fairmile, and urging Cusins to stop Barbara's tongue, Walker goes off.

Barbara leaves Cusins and her father for a while. They begin to discuss the sincerity of Cusins in being a member of the Army and then turn to religion. For Undershaft, religion is money and gunpowder and the virtues conventionally prized (justice, truth, honor), the luxuries of a strong and safe life. Cusins points out that Undershaft will have to choose between that religion and Barbara's. Cusins sympathizes with the Army for having taken a poor professor of Greek like himself and inspired him with the joy of a great cause. And, he adds, he will — poor as he is — marry Barbara; that is settled! His frankness wins Undershaft, just as Undershaft appeals to Cusins' sense of ironic humor; and they both agree now they have a common aim, to win Barbara, a savior of souls, to the side of the millionaire and the poet-professor. When Cusins points out that Barbara and he are in love with the common people, Undershaft coldly rebukes him in a speech pointing out that the love of poverty, dirt, disease, and suffering is an unnatural passion and such love has no romance for him, who was once a poor man. No, he and Cusins and Barbara, he says, must stand together and elevate the common people. And they must begin by making Barbara forsake the Army, if not by persuasion, then by money.

Barbara comes back with Snobby, Shirley, and Jenny, and counts out the money they have taken in at the other gate of the shelter. When Undershaft offers to add to the collection, Barbara turns aside his offer of even a few pennies, saying that she cannot accept money made in his way (by munitions) and that he must work out, not buy, his salvation. All the same, she wishes the Army had thousands with which to do its proper work of saving souls and not have to spend all its energies in getting money.

Enter Bill Walker again, with the story of how Fairmile refused to fight him but made him pray. Now he wants to give money to the Army to make up for having hurt Jenny and wants none of her Christian forgiveness that so unnerves him. But Barbara wants nothing less than his soul and will take no money, declaring the Army will not be bought either by him or her father. Mrs. Baines, an Army Commissioner, comes into the yard and is introduced to Undershaft. She enthusiastically describes the work the Army is doing among the workers, taking away their bitterness and dissatisfaction (Undershaft ironically thanks her for this, but she does not appreciate his wit), and tells of the offer by Lord Saxmundham, or Bodger, the manufacturer of Bodger's whiskey, to contribute five-thousand pounds to the Army if someone will match his offer. Will Undershaft? He will, and writes a check as Walker mutters to Barbara, "What price Salvation now?"

Barbara protests taking tainted money, while Mrs. Baines is carried away by the force of Undershaft's clever, seductive arguments in favor of his contribution, and Cusins, inspired by a spirit of mischief, begins to beat the drum in preparation for the big meeting of celebration that is to take place shortly. Quietly Barbara removes the badge of her office and pins it on her father, as payment for his charity, and says she not only will not accompany the parade but may never pray again. The others march out to music, and Barbara is left with Shirley, Rummy, and Walker. He is angered by the discovery that the money he threw down when Barbara refused it has been taken by Snobby, and he hurls a mug at Rummy for laughing at him. Barbara wants to return the money out of her own pocket; but Walker will not have it, saying he will not be bought and she will not have his soul either. He doesn't believe in any of her talk, he says, and today he has seen how futile is the Army's belief in anything but power and money. Then he leaves, and it is Shirley who tries console the despairing Barbara.

Comment

This act is very rich in contrasts of character. Much of it is in Cockney dialect (Walker, Rummy, Snobby), and we see different kinds of people among the poor: Snobby, a hypocrite like Rummy, taking advantage of the Army's approval of the easy path to salvation through public confessions of sinfulness; Peter Shirley, a broken and gentle man who has some dignity and many mistaken ideas, by Undershaft's views — he says he prefers a good conscience to an empty pocket; and Bill Walker, a bully who is made ashamed by the Army, holds out against its humiliation of him, and is glad to see Barbara lose her faith in her mission. (See Shaw's analysis of Walker in the preface). Undershaft is consistent in his flaunting of poverty as the way of the meek and blessed and knows that a virtuous life can be protected only by power and money. He does not worship evil, but he is true to his profession. Cusins at the close of this act is a little lightheaded and giddy, caught up in an ecstasy of love for Barbara and for his new found calling, and exhilarated by Undershaft's playing the role of the Devil in trying to buy the Army. The climax of the act is Barbara's taking off her badge and sadly pinning it on her father. One hears the cynical question of Walker, "What price Salvation now?"

ACT THREE

Setting

Lady Britomat's library; then Undershaft's factory and town at Perivale St. Andrews.

In Lady Brit's library, Barbara (no longer in uniform), sits with her mother, Sarah, Lomax, and then Cusins, who comes in and tells of the Army meeting and of the night of carousing he has had with Undershaft. Barbara warns him not to let himself be completely won over by her father, whom Cusins humorously calls The Prince of Darkness. Now the butler announces Undershaft, and he and Lady Brit discuss their family affairs in private. She is especially concerned about Stephen, in whom Undershaft has no interest and whom he thinks incapable of heading the cannon foundry. Besides, the Undershaft tradition is against it; a foundling must be discovered to succeeed him, and Undershaft now admits he has been unable to find anyone of merit, a poor boy strong enough of will and mind to resist conventional teaching and make his own way on the strength of his own ideas. Her father is even willing to marry Barbara to such a man, if he can be found, which makes Lady Brit more and more impatient.

Stephen appears at the library door and is drawn into the discussion. He has no taste for business, even a cannon foundry, he says, and reproaches his mother for continuing to treat him as a child that cannot make up its mind. Undershaft questions him now as to the profession he might like to enter, promising him a start in it in return for having disinherited him. But Stephen cannot choose; the only knowledge he claims to possess is that of right and wrong. This sentiment earns Undershaft's laughter, for respectable people who know nothing always claim the knowledge of this most difficult matter. Possibly a career in government, then, on which he lectures his son for failing to realize that Lazarus and Undershaft, the makers of money and possessors of power, are the true rulers of England. Undershaft tries to speak realistically and Stephen replies only in second-hand, high-sounding phrases. Undershaft says he must have a career in journalism, then, where he can make phrases happily.

The others return to the library, preparing to leave on a trip to Undershaft's factory. Barbara thinks it is an infernal, smoke-filled place where the workers are driven to their task, and is surprised to hear Undershaft describe it as a clean and beautiful hillside town, where all needs are provided for and discipline is kept by taking advantage of the native English instinct for keeping ranks of order among the workers. Barbara tells him she can never forgive him for buying the Army and so losing for her the soul of a man (Walker) on the verge of repentance and salvation. But Undershaft urges her not to despair. He argues that she has left her mark on Walker and he will not be lost, though she cannot see it at the moment. This cheers Barbara and appeals to Cusins as a clever argument of the Devil.

The scene changes to Perivale St. Andrews and Undershaft's model factory, where Barbara is standing on a platform overlooking the town. Cusins comes up the path to her, admiring the perfection of the place and commenting on the new job they have found here for Peter Shirley. Then Stephen arrives, filled with enthusiasm for all he has seen here — the libraries, the schools, the hospitals. When Undershaft emerges from his office nearby, Stephen compliments him on the place, and Undershaft says it is all the consequence of organization and planning, with responsibility built in and anxiety left out. Bilton the foreman comes out of an explosives shed to complain of Lomax' carelessness with matches, and then Lady Brit arrives, thoroughly impressed with the domestic arrangements of the town and unhappy about Undershaft's wish to deprive the family of it all. She even proposes Cusins now as successor to Undershaft, but there is the objection that Cusins is not a foundling. But Cusins himself removes that objection now by revealing that by English law his parents, both Australians, are not legally married because his mother is the sister of his father's first wife (Deceased Wife's Sister Act) and so Cusins is illegitimate by that law, hence a foundling. All are astounded by this news, and Undershaft is thoughtful. Cusins is eligible and his mind has not been destroyed, he claims, by public-school instruction in Greek. He is repelled by the business of munitions but willing to head the factory if he can strike the right bargain about wages with Undershaft. This the two men proceed to do, with Cusins showing an aptitude for figures surprising in a professor of Greek. Now Undershaft insists that Cusins as successor in the firm will have to keep the true faith of an armorer, which he describes: Sell weapons at an honest price to all men, and do not judge their persons or principle. This Cusins must agree to, especially when, as their agreement provides, he one day changes his name to Andrew Undershaft.

Undershaft now defends his creed. Ordinary morality means nothing to him in the face of a practical job to be done. And he advises Barbara, if she is disappointed and shaken in her former belief that souls can be saved by the power of religion instead of by Lazarus and Undershaft, to scrap her old way of thinking and get a new one, as he has always done when necessary. There is light here in the model town, he argues, and darkness and despair at the Army shelter. Cleanliness and self-respect save souls, and he has saved Barbara's by letting her grow up protected by them, and in addition he has saved her from the worst crime of all — poverty. Bring Bill Walker here and he will save even him with better housing, food, and clothing. Undershaft says that he himself was determined to avoid poverty and would rather have been a thief than a pauper and a murderer with his machine guns than a slave receiving Christian charity and sermons on humility and resignation. As for munitions making, whoever is brave enough to blow up men, can change society more effectively than parliamentary government. What does Cusins say? Will he subscribe to the faith of the armorer? Cusins hesitates, Lady Brit is shocked by her husband's arguments,

Barbara is uncertain. And Cusins too, who wonders if there is no place for pity, love, forgiveness in that creed. Besides, he is divided in his mind, wanting to work with Undershaft and yet fearful of losing Barbara. And he hates war. Then make war on war, says Undershaft, and use the weapons around him. He then escorts his wife and the children on a tour of the guncotton sheds, leaving Barbara and Cusins to consider his offer.

Cusins tells her he will accept Undershaft's faith and work for reality and power after years of selling his soul for small gains like professorships and security. Barbara replies that she is interested in power, too, spiritual power. That is what all power is, he says; and the power of weapons is a power for good as well as evil, and has never been abused, as the power of religion or intellect or imagination has, to keep common men slaves to politicians, teachers, and pretentious fools of all kinds. And now Barbara agrees he has made the right decision, for she has come to see that her work in the Army was misdirected and that turning her back on Undershaft was turning her back on life. She maintains that life is all of one piece and evil must be endured, not moralized about. She will have no class from now on and will give herself to working for Undershaft's model town, saving the souls of well-fed men and women, who are the only kinds to do God's work. And so her faith in her work is restored, she has returned to the colors with a new, better mission and is again Major Barbara.

Comment

This last act concentrates the main issues of the play and moves from social comedy in the first half (Lady Brit's library) to an intensive consideration of social questions and personal faith in the second half (Undershaft's factory). Undershaft's interview with Stephen is wittily executed, as the young man reveals himself a pillar of conventional morality, unfit for any profession except journalism, that of elaborate word-mongering and half-truth telling. In the factory scene Shaw lets Undershaft explain himself fully as he recites the faith of the armorer. His beliefs appear to the superficial as crudely materialistic and dedicated to destructiveness. What must be appreciated is that Undershaft is realistic and hardheaded about society, refusing to accept remedies for social ills that fail to be radical. He believes bodies are to be saved first and souls afterward, or that saving the body is saving the soul. Poverty to him is a crime because it destroys both. As a maker of weapons he believes he has the potential power to make war on war when men are ready to do so, and he will not moralize about his profession. Cusins is attracted by power, intoxicated by the thought that he can use it for good purposes. His disclosure that he is in one sense a foundling is a piece of theatrical surprise, artificial and belonging to the conventions of farce. But it solves the problem of succession. There is suspense in his making a decision about Undershaft's offer. The audience asks: Will he take the job and lose the girl? Or give up the job for the girl? He makes his decision first, note, then asks Barbara what she will do. A change has taken place in her upon seeing the town and listening to her father, the old Prince of Darkness, and she approves Cusins' becoming the next Andrew Undershaft.

ANALYSIS OF SELECTED CHARACTERS

Barbara

She is warm, sympathetic, not at all conventional or rigid, only misguided. She has to learn that social conditions are responsible for the plight of the people she wants to save, and that to save them with a piece of bread in one hand and a Bible in the other is sheer hypocrisy. She makes some impression on Bill Walker and loses him along with her faith in herself, because she does not understand that her father and the distillers of whiskey are the true powers of the world. She has a half-mystical belief in a higher principle than that of guns and money; and when she learns that the well-fed and well-housed, not the unfortunate and the desperate, are the best material for salvation then she is ready and happy to do God's work.

Andrew Undershaft

A defier of ordinary ways of thinking, he is considered by some a disciple of the Devil. And indeed he is, if by that is meant that he will not accept the morality that keeps men enslaved. He distresses Lady Brit by rejecting the proper life she approves and by being original in everything he does. He undermines the faith Barbara has in her mission only to restore it after he has taught her to think freshly. He is witty, quick, perceptive, shrewd, compassionate but unsentimental, and has a profound faith in the creed he has adopted.

Adolphus (Dolly) Cusins

He is a professor of Greek, an educated man, with an ironic sense of humor that mocks others as well as himself. He has the temperament of a poet: as in Act Two he quotes a long passage of Euripides, the ancient Greek playwright, with additions of his own; and has a keen sense of the ideal. He is hesitant and uncertain about allying himself with a dealer in destruction like Undershaft, but he is drawn by the prospect of using power. He defends himself by joking and raillery from the searching implications of Undershaft's philosophy until his defenses are broken by the older man's unrelenting logic. He joins the Salvation Army to be near Barbara, yet confesses to a belief in something beyond himself. His final decision is to work for the common man against the authorities of the world that have held him down with false promises and pretentious misinformation about the way the world is run.

Lady Britomart

Her name is roughly sympolic of England (Britain) and in character that is what she is. She is a crusty matron who keeps her family in hand by continuously invoking the household gods of decent order and respectability. But she is not inflexible and is in many ways an attractive character. Note the way she puts down the foolish Charles Lomax, whose childish style of speaking, fuzziness of mind exasperate her. The "weak" characters of the play, Lomax and Sarah and Stephen, are no match for her, and the stronger characters. Barbara, Cusins, Undershaft defer politely and affectionately to her. She has an aristocratic sense of what is fitting and proper, but this does not prevent her from being enthusiastic, for all her disagreement with her husband's views, about his experimental town for workers.

PYGMALION: A ROMANCE IN FIVE ACTS (1912)

INTRODUCTION

In a Greek legend, Pygmalion, a sculptor and ruler of Cyprus, was known for his dislike of women. But when he had carved an ivory statue of the goddess Aphrodite, its charms so overhelmed him that he fell in love with it. The goddess answered his prayer to bring the statue to life, and he married the women it contained, who was then named Galatea. Shaw's play is a variation on this legend, with Professor Higgins as Pygmalion and Eliza Doolittle as Galatea. The review of the play that follows adheres to the text found in the edition of complete plays and not to the "reading version" which incorporates scenes Shaw wrote for the 1938 film of *Pygmalion.*

CHARACTERS

PROFESSOR HENRY HIGGINS	A confirmed bachelor, about forty; a professor of phonetics.
ELIZA DOOLITTLE	A Cockney flower girl, under twenty.
ALFRED DOOLITTLE	Eliza's father, a dustman (trash collector).
COLONEL PICKERING	Friend of Higgins; a retired officer.
FREDDY EYNSFORD-HILL	A pleasant young man of the upper class.
MRS. EYNSFORD-HILL	His mother.

MISS CLARA EYNSFORD-HILL	His sister.
MRS. HIGGINS	Henry Higgins' mother.
MRS. PEARCE	Higgins' housekeeper.

PARLORMAID, A BYSTANDER, and PEDESTRIANS at Covent Garden in Act I.

Preface

This preface has little to do with the play, and Shaw saves his remarks on that for the section he calls the sequel to *Pygmalion* (see below, following Act V). The prefatory material is mostly a description of Henry Sweet, a professor of phonetics at Oxford, touches of whom are in the characterization of Higgins in this play.

ACT ONE

Setting

Covent Garden, after the theatre. The porch of St. Paul's Church, during a heavy summer rain.

An assorted group of people stands in the porch of St. Paul's, huddling there in protection against a sudden and heavy rainstorm. Mrs. Eynsford-Hill and her daughter Clara look impatiently for Freddy Eynsford-Hill, whom they have sent to find a cab. When he returns without one, they, complaining, send him off again, and as he goes off a second time he collides with a flower girl (Liza or Eliza) and spills her basket of wares. She calls after him familiarly, quite by accident hitting upon his correct first name, then sits on the curb to rearrange her flowers. Mrs. Eynsford-Hill, who has overheard their very brief exchange and misunderstands it, wishes to know how this poorly dressed and badly washed girl, with a thick Cockney accent, comes to know her son, and so buys some flowers from her, over Clara's protest. The flower girl explains, just as an elderly military-looking gentleman (Pickering) rushes to the shelter of the porch. The girl tries to sell him a flower. He refuses her, but gives her some small change anyway. She is warned against taking the money by a bystander, who says there is a man taking notes of everything she says. The girl is alarmed, fearing she will be reported by a detective to the police and accused of addressing gentlemen for immoral purposes; she begins to cry out and attract the attention of everyone in the shelter of the porch.

Now the notetaker (Professor Higgins) turns and tells her to be quiet, then reads off in phonetic Cockney what she has been saying. Others intervene and tell him to leave the girl alone. But the notetaker asks the girl a number of questions that suggest he knows where she was born and where she comes from, and he surprises some of the others, especially the elderly gentleman, by telling them their locality. He does the same for the Eynsford-Hills, to the annoyance of Clara, and then offers to find then a cab. But the rain has stopped now, and mother and daughter make for the bus nearby as other pedestrians move off, leaving the elderly-gentleman, the flower girl, and the notetaker.

Now the notetaker discloses that his profession is phonetics, the science of speech, and that he makes his living by improving the accents of socially ambitious people. He can, for example, take in hand this flower girl (all the while complaining in "awful-sounding" Cockney) and in three months' time pass her off as a duchess at an ambassador's garden party. Now the elderly gentleman introduces himself as Colonel Pickering, author of Spoken Sanscrit, and the notetaker proves to be Henry Higgins, author of Higgins' Universal Alphabet. Each knows the other's work and wanted to meet. They go off to discuss their interest in speech, but Higgins first throws the flower girl some money. Freddy returns, having found a cab, but now the ladies have gone. No matter. The flower girl sweeps by him and hires the cab for herself with the money she has got that evening, leaving Freddy astonished and wondering.

Comment

The primary interest of the audience in this act is usually in Higgins' performance (almost a theatrical one, it is remarked). His identification of people by their accents makes him seem a man of mysterious powers, and Shaw cleverly delays telling us who he is, a professor of speech, until the last minutes of the act. We see some traits of his character too: he tends to be impatient and heedless of feelings, unsentimental. There is some humor in his bullying of the flower girl, his mimicking of her ugly speech, just as there is in the contrast between her appearance and language and the elegance she affects at the end when taking a cab.

ACT TWO

Setting

Higgins' laboratory-drawing-room. Eleven o'clock the next morning.

In his laboratory, which doubles as a living room, Higgins is giving Colonel Pickering a demonstration of the methods and equipment he uses to discriminate vowel sounds. Mrs. Pearce, the housekeeper, enters to announce disapprovingly that a common young woman wants to see the professor. He is puzzled, but decides it will be instructive to record her voice, if she has an unusual accent, and so asks Mrs. Pearce to admit her. The girl who now enters is the flower girl, tidied up and loudly dressed and trying to appear businesslike. Higgins is annoyed and disappointed, Pickering somehow touched by the girl, whom he treats gently in the conversation that follows, whereas Mrs. Pearce scolds her for putting on airs and Higgins thunders and bullies her. Her name is Liza Doolittle, she says, and she has come to ask Higgins to give her speech lessons so that she may obtain a job in a flower shop once her speech is ladylike and genteel. She heard him say last night that he was not above giving lessons, and she is ready to pay all of a shilling an hour, which amuses and interests Higgins, who figures that the sum is a large portion of her daily small income. Pickering is interested too; he makes a wager, all the expenses of the experiment, that Higgins can't do what he spoke of the night before, pass this girl off as a duchess at an ambassador's garden party. Higgins considers, then decides on the spur of the moment. He will do it in six months, in three if Liza is quick enough, and he orders Mrs. Pearce to take away Liza's clothing, clean her up and give her new things to wear. The girl is outraged at this and Mrs. Pearce asks him to consider the wisdom of his action; Eliza must have parents or may be married. Higgins now tries to be winning to Eliza, half mocking her, though, with the description of the young men who will certainly want to marry her when he has transformed her. Eliza thinks his talk is crazy and starts to leave, then changes her mind and comes back. Mrs. Pearce persists. Though the girl says she has no parents and is not married, still there is the question of what basis she is to live on in this house. Will Higgins pay her? And what is to become of her once the experiment is finished? But Higgins' answers are only half serious, and he refuses to consider consequences. Resigned to his ways, Mrs. Pearce takes Eliza from the room.

Pickering, though, follows up the housekeeper's questions. He makes Higgins, who confesses himself unable to deal with women, assure him there will be no attempt to take advantage of Eliza's position. Mrs. Pearce comes back into the room to ask Higgins to please be careful about his language before Eliza, and to mind his boorish table manners. He promises to do as she wishes, and she goes out, only to return in a moment and announce that a Mr. Alfred Doolittle, a dustman, is at the door, making inquiries about his daughter. Pickering anticipates trouble, but Higgins seems to relish a fight and asks that Doolittle be sent up.

But there is no quarrel, first because Higgins cleverly disarms Doolittle by acting as though he is ready to give Eliza over to him at once if he should choose to play the outraged father, and second because *Doolittle* is such an engaging rascal that he manages to throw Higgins off his guard. He had discovered from a neighborhood child that Eliza was here and has come with her luggage. All he wants is five pounds for her on which he proposes to have a spree with his common-law wife. Higgins is so taken with the dustman's attack on hypocritical middle-class morality and the defense of his rights as a member of what he calls the undeserving poor that he wants to double the money Doolittle asks. But Doolittle will not have it, arguing that too much money would make him cautious and destroy his enjoyment. And finally with the money in hand, about to leave, he nearly collides with a young woman entering the room in a Japanese kimono. He does not recognize Eliza, who speaks of him critically after he has gone and begins to talk snobbishly.

Higgins warns her of her old friends. But she doesn't care, and when Mrs. Pearce says that new clothes have come for her to try on, she rushes out excitedly.

Comment

The most arresting and amusing character in this second act is Alfred Doolittle. His arrival provides a fresh turn in the action and a bit of suspense when we hear that he is Eliza's father. His scene with Higgins is built on the principle of reversal. That is, from his determination not to be taken advantage of, we expect the strong-minded Higgins to triumph. But Doolittle so delights him with his unconventional opinions that Higgins is completely won over and is soon offering the man twice what he has asked. Doolittle's speech on middle-class morality may seem slightly out of place in this play, somewhat forced into its context; but that is chiefly because we have come to think of this play, such an immense success as a musical comedy, *My Fair Lady,* as being not completely typical of Shaw in its themes. But see the discussion below of the sequel, and consider Higgins' remarks all through the play about the inconsistencies and ironies of prevailing social conditions.

ACT THREE

Setting

The drawing-room of Mrs. Higgins. Between 4 and 5 PM.

Waiting for guests to visit her on her receiving (at home) day, Mrs. Higgins is distressed when her son Henry bursts into her drawing room and asks her to receive a flower girl he has picked up and trained to speak correctly. Her son's manners put people off and she wishes he would go away. But he is preoccupied with Eliza, congratulating her rapid progress in pronunciation and complaining that it is *what* she says that is the problem; therefore he has instructed her to limit her conversation to the neutral topics of weather and health.

He is on the point of going when the parlormaid announces Mrs. and Miss Eynsford-Hill whom Higgins faintly remembers from their accent but cannot place. Then Pickering comes in and Higgins, who has been indifferent to the company, is cheered at the prospect of a larger group for Eliza to meet. Freddy arrives and greets the other men in his fashionable indolent manner of speaking. Soon the parlormaid announces Eliza, beautifully dressed and having an air of great self-possession. In the scene that follows she speaks as she had been warned, only on her set topics. Of the weather she speaks with such killing precision that Freddy is instantly amused. On health, she tells of the sensational death of her aunt, at some length and in a style that mixes carefully correct grammar with lower class slang and that surprises the ladies. Higgins hastily excuses the slang as "the new small talk," but soon he makes a discreet signal to Eliza and she gets up to leave. Freddy, completely smitten by her unusual charm, offers to accompany her, but she chooses to leave alone and he goes out on the balcony to catch another look at her. Mrs. Eynsford-Hill comments unfavorably on the new way of speaking, but Clara is quite taken with it and at Higgins' mischievous suggestion promises to try it out on other people. She and her mother leave and are followed by Freddy, who confusedly hopes he will see Miss Doolittle again at Mrs. Higgins' home.

Higgins and Pickering are pleased with Eliza's first test in polite society, but Mrs. Higgins is not, pointing out that the girl gives herself away in every sentence and that mostly because she has unwittingly copied Henry's brusque way of talking. She inquires into arrangements at her son's house, and is assured that everything is proper there. Higgins adds that Eliza has become very useful in helping around the house, and he compliments himself on having devoted so much attention to her training and this most interesting experiment that will bring one class closer to another. He and Pickering break into an enthusiastic praise of Eliza's quickness at learning new things, including music, cutting across each other's remarks until Mrs. Higgins has to quiet them both. Soberly she tries to get them to consider the same question Mrs. Pearce had asked earlier: What is to happen to Eliza after the lessons are finished? What is she to do? When is she to go? There is no worse fate than having an education that puts her above her station but does not provide her with the income to keep up her new position. But the men answer her vaguely and generally, Higgins promising to find some light employment for Eliza. They then leave in high spirits over their success, and Mrs. Higgins, bothered by their indifference and unable to go back to letter writing, exclaims, "Oh, men! men!! men!!!"

Comment

In this act Eliza-Galatea begins to come to life, a woman emerging gradually from the work of art Higgins-Pygmalion is so proud of having made. But so far she has come only half to life. Mrs. Higgins is concerned about the future of this "living doll" (Mrs. Higgins' words) that amuses her son and Pickering. She points to the genteel poverty of the well-bred Eynsford-Hills as an example of what lies in store for a girl who has not the means to keep up a new social position. Eliza has impressed the naive Clara and made a conquest of Freddy in a deliciously comic scene (in the 1938 film version of the play, in the reading version, and in the musical comedy, it is in this scene that Shaw has her make the famous observation that "The rain in Spain stays mainly in the plains."); but the serious problem of what to do later with Eliza remains.

ACT FOUR

Setting

Higgins' laboratory. Twelve o'clock on a summer night.

The voices of Pickering and Higgins are heard in the hall, then Eliza comes from the landing into the laboratory. She is beautifully dressed in evening clothes and is very tired as she sits dispiritedly on the piano bench. Pickering and Higgins enter, conversing, and Higgins looks about for his slippers. He does not find them at first, and because he barely notices Eliza, he does not see her leave and return to place the slippers at his feet on the hearth. She sits as before and listens to the two men review the evening's events. Eliza has been a great success at the garden party, then at dinner and later at the opera. But now Higgins confesses he has been bored by the whole experiment, and especially so when he saw he would easily win his bet. Pickering comments on the really professional style in which Eliza deported herself, and saying goodnight, goes up to bed. Higgins prepares to go up too and turns to tell Eliza to put out the lights. This is too much for her. When he turns back for his slippers, she hurls them at him and astounds him with a show of anger. She calls him a selfish brute who would throw her back in the gutter now that she has won his bet for him, and she attacks him physically and has to be restrained by Higgins. She keeps lamenting her lot, asking repeatedly what is to become of her. Higgins tries to comfort her, moderating his tone, to assure her she is suffering from nerves. He suggests that she will not have a hard time finding somewhere to go, something to do; she might even marry after all, not all men are perennial bachelors like himself and the Colonel. Pleased with his advice, he takes up an apple from the dessert stand and eats it. Quietly, Eliza informs him she is not for sale to any man who happens to fancy her, and says she wishes he had left her where he found her. Higgins then reminds her of the flower shop she wanted to open and of the possibility of Pickering's setting her up in it. But Eliza is not receptive to this idea. She is deeply offended by his cool behavior and asks him to define what has been bought for her as part of the experiment and what she may keep. Higgins says all the clothing they have purchased is hers, if that's the ungrateful way she feels, but not the hired jewelry. When she offers to return a ring he has bought for her, he angrily throws it into the fireplace, and she sees that she has wounded him. Higgins is furious and tries not to show that she has somehow got at him where it hurts, but when he leaves the room he cannot help slamming the door savagely behind him, calling her "a heartless guttersnipe." Alone, Eliza smiles at **her triumph,** does a mocking imitation of Higgins' exit, and then searches for the ring he has thrown down.

Comment

The statue has come fully to life and in this act has revealed a soul. Eliza suffers from Higgins' indifference to her fate, from the casual way he and Pickering discuss her. She wants to hurt him, to get back "some of her own," and she does so by making him lose his temper and show that he can be hurt himself even if he has no respect for the feelings of others. Thematically, this act repeats the question of the earlier one: What is to become of a newly manufactured duchess who cannot go back to selling flowers on the streets?

ACT FIVE

Setting

Mrs. Higgins' drawing room. The next morning.

The parlormaid comes in to tell Mrs. Higgins that the professor and the Colonel are downstairs and telephoning the police. They are, it turns out, looking for Eliza, who has disappeared, having left Higgins' house early that morning. They do not know that Eliza is upstairs, where, Mrs. Higgins instructs, she is to remain until sent for. Higgins and the Colonel are upset and distracted when they come in, Higgins especially put out by the inconvenience of Eliza's sudden leave-taking. She has kept his appointments in order and done him small services.

They are interrupted by the appearance of someone the maid announces as a Mr. Doolittle, a gentleman. Thinking this might be some relation of Eliza's they have not met and to whom she might have gone, the two men are eager to meet him. He comes up, and proves to be Alfred Doolittle again, now dressed in formal clothing. His luck has changed, he has come into a great deal of money, but he is not happy. He reproaches Higgins with having delivered him over to middle-class morality. In a spirit of fun, Higgins had given Doolittle's name to an American millionaire in search of England's most original moralist, and in his will this man has left money in trust as long as Doolittle agrees to lecture up to six times a year on moral reform! Doolittle complains of having lost his old lower-class comforts and of being forced into a new confining respectability. It is too much to expect him to give up the money, so there he is, trapped. Mrs. Higgins sees this new wealth as a solution to the problem of Eliza's future, but Henry protests that he bought Eliza from Doolittle and will not allow her father to interfere now. Mrs. Higgins discloses that Eliza is upstairs, scorns the heartless treatment of the girl by her son and the Colonel, and offers to have Eliza come down if Henry will watch his manners. She requests Mr. Doolittle to retire for a moment to the balcony.

When she comes in, Eliza is very calm, assured, dignified. She sits down and takes up a piece of needlework and does not allow herself to be rattled by Higgins' attempts to treat her as a piece of property or a creature he has made. Instead she addresses herself to Pickering, thanks him for the kind and gentlemanly way he has always treated her, never like a flower girl and always like a lady — and that, she says, is what makes the difference between the two, not how a girl behaves but how she is treated. She can always learn how to dress properly, and a Higgins can teach her to speak correctly, but a Pickering with good manners and gentleness can give her the self-respect that makes her forever a lady and nevermore a flower girl. She says in answer to the Colonel's invitation that she can not go back to Higgins' place in Wimpole Street, to which Higgins retorts that without him she will relapse in three weeks and go back to the gutter. No, says Eliza, the lesson has been well learned, and she does not believe she could utter any of the old sounds again.

But suddenly Doolittle, in the room again, touches her on the shoulder and she emits a long-drawn Cockney howl that delights Higgins. Doolittle tells Eliza that he is to marry her stepmother that morning and asks his daughter to attend. When she leaves the room a moment to get ready, Doolittle confesses to the men that he has never told Eliza that he was not married to her mother either. Pickering and Mrs. Higgins will come to the ceremony too. Eliza returns and says again she will not go back to Wimpole Street, a matter, says her father, in which he will not interfere.

The wedding party leaves, except Eliza, because Higgins stands before the door and will not let her pass. Now they have it out. Higgins wants her to come back, but he tells her he will not change for anyone. He is not a snob; he is like her father in that he will treat a duchess as he would a flower girl and a flower girl as a duchess, if he likes. He tells. Eliza he will indeed miss her, that he has grown accustomed to her voice and appearance. To which she replies that he has both, in photographs and recordings, if he should ever feel lonely. But it is her soul he will miss; he is concerned for life and humanity. He wants no more slipper-fetching from her, he wants no affection, he wants fellowship and a friendly relationship in the pleasant old way that he and she and Pickering enjoyed. He will adopt her, if she likes, settle money on her, and he will not see her thrown away on Freddy Eynsford-Hill, who, she now discloses, has been writing her romantic letters. She wants kindness and love from somebody. Higgins wants only to be natural. Eliza does not know which way to turn: She is reluctant to go back to Wimpole Street, she can never go back to Covent Garden, and she will not live with her father. But she will have independence all the same. She thinks she has answer. She will teach. Teach what? Higgins wants to know. What he taught her — phonetics. Didn't he once say she had a better ear than his own? And she will begin by working with one of his competitors. This is too much for Higgins, who threatens to wring her neck if she goes near the man, and lays hands on her. This is Eliza's second great moment (the first was her wounding of him in Act IV), and she defies him, telling him to wring away, she knew someday he would strike her! This is the way to get at him, not to be afraid of him. Higgins admires her, preferring this behavior to snivelling and crying for affection and being his servant.

Mrs. Higgins comes in to say the carriage is waiting for Eliza. Higgins, who is too unruly in church, must stay behind. Very cheerful and self-satisfied, Higgins gives the departing Eliza a few little errands to perform, thinking he has settled their quarrel and that she will come back and be a jolly old bachelor like him and Pickering. But Eliza refuses him. Mrs. Higgins fears Henry has spoiled her. But Higgins reassures her that Eliza will do as he asks.

SEQUEL

The play may *seem* to end in a somewhat unresolved fashion, but Shaw explains himself in the pages that follow the last act of the drama. There will, he writes, be no "happy ending" of the usual sort, even though *Pygmalion* is a romance (the word refers to Eliza's exceedingly improbable transformation from guttersnipe to duchess); Eliza will not marry Higgins simply to satisfy the sentimentalists and so spoil the drama. Eliza's decision is a firm one; she is young enough to find her way in the world, and though she will not marry the professor, she will keep him as a friend because she has a strong interest in him and he in her. There are other reasons for not marrying him: he is more than twenty years her senior; she knows intuitively that no other woman can win him because his mother is an "irresistible rival" owing to her wealth, charm, intelligence; and Eliza does not want to be an interest secondary to that he takes in his work; she will always resent his superior way with her, his clever attempts to coax her and evade her anger after he has bullied her.

But Shaw says Eliza did marry Freddy, which should not be a surprise to anyone. She could cope with him and eventually with the economic difficulties their marriage brought. His mother was too poor to help them, and Doolittle, having risen even more in the world, found he was spending too much to be able to help out. It was the Colonel who rescued them. He helped the young couple open a flower shop, continued his support when they got into financial difficulties, and gently tried to keep the peace when Higgins became too openly amused at the idea of Freddy's doing any real work.

But at last, under their great effort, the business began to prosper, and soon they were in a position to do without Pickering's aid. Eliza, Shaw concludes, is still influential in Wimpole Street. She gets along with Higgins as well as she can, loves the colonel, and defends Freddy against Higgins' derision. She is sure that Higgins never really meant it when he told her he would miss her if she left. She knows he is self-absorbed and yet not selfish in a common way. But he makes her uncomfortable, the relation of Pygmalion to Galatea being "too godlike to be altogether agreeable."

Comment Act V And Sequel

> Act V provides another confrontation of Eliza and Higgins, continuing and resolving that begun in Act IV. Higgins is as rude and unfeeling to everyone else as he is to her (notice his brusqueness with his and the Eynsford-Hills). Because he is no respecter of classes, he is like her father, thinks Eliza. All of this to Higgins is a sign of strength. But Eliza wants to be loved and respected.

She cannot fully appreciate his argument that she has a soul and so must be above such trivial considerations. Her plea is touching, but Higgins wants her to avoid self-sympathy. And he wants to get round her. For a moment she is almost taken in by his appearing to soften and become human, then realizes she is not much more important to him than his carpet slippers, or if she is, it is only as a proof of his skill in creating a work of artifice. Because they are essentially incompatible, Shaw rejects the ordinary coming together of lovers at the end of a comedy. His play, he implies, is above easy and secondhand inventions. His interest, too, is in his social, not his romantic, themes. He enjoys the ironic and to him deeply comic resolutions that he does supply in the place of the happy ending. What are they? (1) The gap between classes is closed by education and, as Higgins argues, there is no difference in human substance or soul between one person and another, only a difference between opportunities; (2) a secondary proof of this is in the subplot of Doolittle's adventures. A dustman at heart and by profession, he rises in society, thanks to a stroke of fortune that belongs to the traditions of farce, and makes a show of his origins that delights his social superiors; (3) there is a third motif in the Eynsford-Hill passages. Freddy is completely taken in by Eliza and genuinely worships her. That she is of humble origins makes him love her all the more. She is much cleverer than Freddy, his patchy middle-class education having fitted him for nothing. At first his mother and Clara are opposed to the opening of the shop, Shaw tells us in the Sequel, but eventually Clara goes into business, gives up her idle pretensions to gentility, is converted to the doctrine of work and self-advancement after reading socialist writings, and becomes a credit to her family and to herself. To repeat: All of this is what interests Shaw in *Pygmalion* and not the false prospect of wedding bells for the hero and heroine. In the film, the ending is ambiguous, the suggestion left that maybe there will be a marriage; in *My Fair Lady,* Higgins seems genuinely repentant, and the audience is led to expect again that there will be a romantic conclusion. But in the original stage version Shaw is more Shavian than his adaptors and improvers.

ANALYSIS OF SELECTED CHARACTERS

HENRY HIGGINS

He is a man dedicated to his work and short of patience with those who disagree or get in his way. He has been so petted and indulged by his charming mother that he will never change his habits, especially that of bachelorhood. He has more than a little touch of the genius figure so frequent in Shaw's plays. He is mocking, eccentric, disrespectful, hostile to fools, attractive to women, moody, devastatingly intelligent, heedless of feelings when they conflict with his own sense of things, a little childlike and childish, a believer in the ideal rationally conceived and worked for, and yet a poet in his own way.

ELIZA

Her beauty and natural dignity are obscured at first by the mud and low speech of Covent Garden. But they are there, just as the ideal figure in the stone waits to be released by the hand of the sculptor. When she comes to life, Higgins has reason to be proud of his handiwork. She exceeds his expectations. She is no match for his caustic wit, but he has unwittingly made of her a splendid human being who is superior to her creator in feeling. He wants to keep her a statue, but by challenging him and making him finally meet her on her own terms, she transforms herself into a person.

ALFRED DOOLITTLE

His characterization contributes to the fairy tale element of the play. His surprising transformation from dustman to the exponent of a new morality is accomplished by the force of his own wit and by the readiness of people to believe in him. Shaw means the Doolittle strand of the plot to be satirical, to make another point about class distinctions (they obscure merit, Eliza's or her father's). And Shaw provides laughter by the gullibility of Doolittle's audience of eager supporters, by the easy success the dustman has in respectable society.

GEORGE BERNARD SHAW

SAINT JOAN

A CHRONICLE PLAY IN SIX SCENES AND AN EPILOGUE (1923)

Introduction

By "chronicle play," Shaw recalls a kind of play popular in the time of Shakespeare that dramatized historical events, usually derived from the reign of an English king (e.g., *Richard III*). *Saint Joan* is a chronicle of some events in the life of Jeanne (or Joan) d'Arc (1412?-1431), a French peasant girl living at the time of the Hundred Years War (1337-1453) between England and France. The English laid claim to French lands and tried to secure them by conquest, provoking a conflict that lasted for over a hundred years, with only short interims of peace. By 1429 the English, with their Burgundian allies, held most of France north of the River Loire. It was in that year that Joan came to the rescue of her country.

CHARACTERS

Joan, The Maid

About seventeen; she says she is inspired by saints to save France.

Robert De Baudricourt

A squire.

Bertrand De Poulengey

A gentleman soldier.

The Archbishop Of Rheims

At the court of the Dauphin of France.

Msgr. De La Tremouille

Lord Chamberlain at the court.

Gilles De Rais

A young courtier known as Bluebeard.

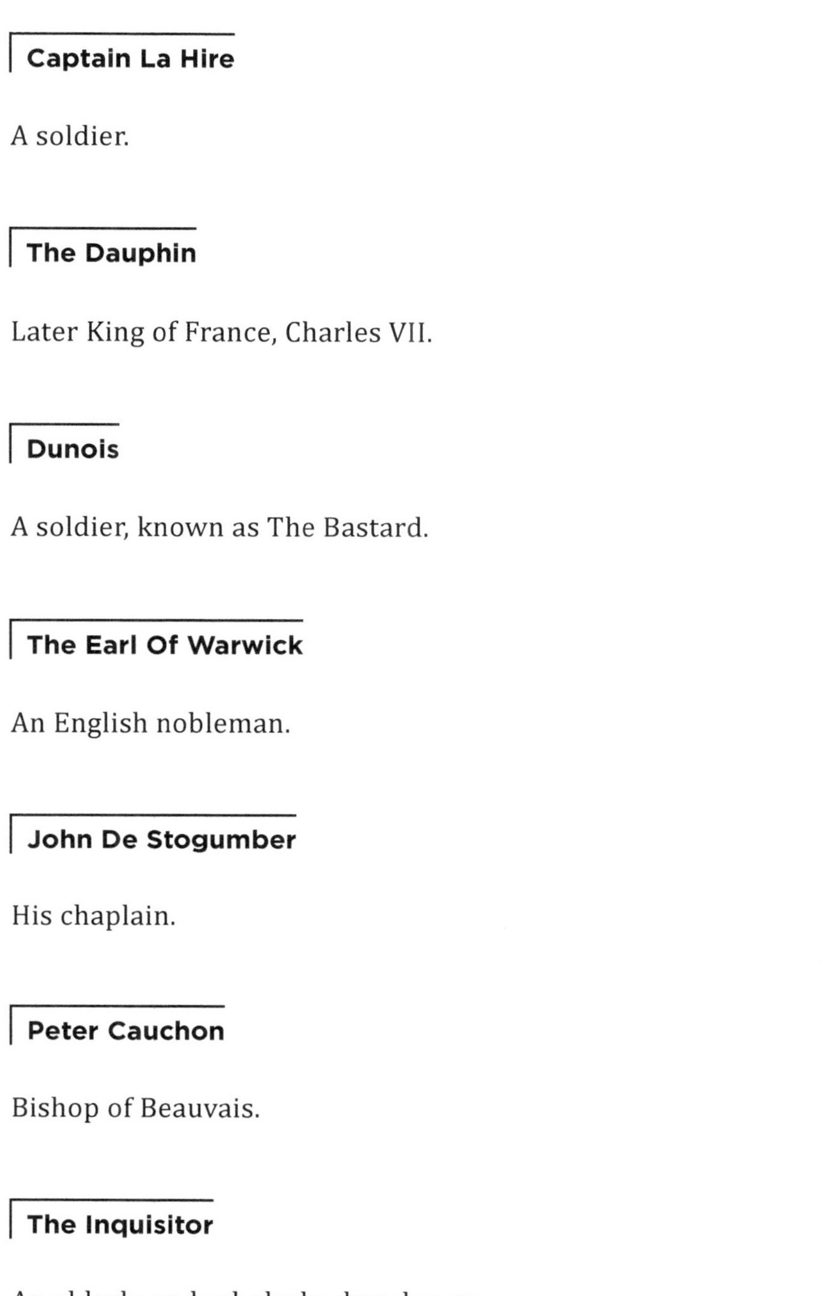

Captain La Hire

A soldier.

The Dauphin

Later King of France, Charles VII.

Dunois

A soldier, known as The Bastard.

The Earl Of Warwick

An English nobleman.

John De Stogumber

His chaplain.

Peter Cauchon

Bishop of Beauvais.

The Inquisitor

An elderly and scholarly churchman.

D'estivet

Prosecutor at Joan's trial.

De Courcelles

A priest at the trial.

Brother Martin Ladvenu

A kindly young monk.

An English Soldier

In the Epilogue.

A Gentleman Of 1920

In the Epilogue.

A Court Page, Warwick's Page, De Baudricourt's Steward, Duchess De La Tremouille, Courtiers, Soldiers, Clerics.

PREFACE

Shaw begins by making a comparison of the historical Joan with the Joan of legend and finds her to have been "one of the first Protestant martyrs." Though necessarily born and raised a Catholic, she followed the dictates of her conscience in defiance of all official authority. She was an innocent who did not appreciate the violent effect she was having on her contemporaries, and she was largely unconscious of her being a genius. Shaw describes her as the plain daughter of a prosperous farmer, unlettered but not ignorant, and in the vexed matter of her voices, sane and not mad or a saint on earth. To him she is more like a person of vision who acted on the claims of her intelligence and imagination. She was, Shaw further argues, a rationalist who used her common sense and courage in the management of military affairs; but the decisions she made she ascribed to the promptings of saints' voices. In the end, her youth and her inexperience of the world, which she thought she could somehow change by the force of her honesty and originality, betrayed her. Unable to comprehend the elaborate structures of medieval society, church, and state, she became a martyr of her inspiration.

The representations of the Maid in world literature are all wanting because they attempt to make her a figure of romance in addition to distorting the picture of her era. Joan's trial for heresy and sorcery was judicially fair. Only Joan did not understand essentially what she was being accused of. She did not perceive that her crime was substituting her unshakable faith in the voices for the advice of ecclesiastical authority in all interpretations of God's will. That the Church reversed its verdict and eventually had Joan canonized as a saint (in 1920, the occasion for the writing of this play) Shaw explains by reference to its history and institutions.

Shaw dismisses as irrelevant the manner of Joan's death (by burning) and finds that modern times are not particularly advanced in humanity. More importantly, the Church of Joan's time was intolerant of private genius. Not that the nineteenth would have supported Joan's rejection of authority either. There must always be a conflict between "genius and discipline" in which genius has to be challenged because it tends to outrun inflexible institutions and vested powers. The real Joan has never been marvelous enough for us. We have never been able to follow the example of her genius, though we have felt free to alter the facts of her character and career.

Shaw discusses the problems of writing an historical play and compares the accomplishment of Shakespeare in this form with his own. In the historical plays, Shaw argues, the Bard did not truly understand the forces that make men express themselves in laws and religions. His stories are personal, about heroes and villains. In *Saint Joan* the reader will find no stage villains but people who act earnestly in the best light of their times. This play is tragedy, not melodrama, and is guilty of no convenient dramatic falsifications of men or events. As for the Epilogue, which is not historical, it was necessary to show Joan canonized, as well as excommunicated and burned, because the play treats not only "the tragedy of her execution" but "the comedy of the attempts of posterity to make amends."

Comment

The preface sets up Joan as another version of the vital reformer who is destroyed by the unbending system. She is much like the man of moral passion and the genius, and her story is tragedy, not comedy. We must remember that Shaw's play, for all its authority and impressive command of historical materials, is but one interpretation of Joan's story. For others in our time, compare Maxwell Anderson's *Joan of Lorraiie* and Jean Anouilh's *The Lark*.

Scene One

Setting

The castle of Vaucouleurs. A spring morning, 1429.

In a chamber of his castle Esquire Robert de Baudricourt is chiding his steward for failure to produce fresh eggs for breakfast. The steward protests that a spell has been laid on the castle and the hens will not lay as long as the Maid is at the door. The girl from Lorraine has been there two days and will not leave until she has had an interview with the Squire. Reluctantly Robert goes to the window and calls her to come up to him. Joan the Maid enters and astonishes him by declaring that the Lord has sent her to gain from him a horse, armor, and soldiers to accompany her to the Dauphin of France. The Dauphin in turn will give her more soldiers with which to raise the English siege of Orleans, and then she will see him crowned King in Rheims Cathedral. All this her voices have told her. Others want to go with her, noblemen like Polly, Bertrand de Poulengey, whom the Squire now sends for after dismissing Joan.

The two men briefly review the political and military situation. The English hold Paris and France itself to the Loire River, and the Dauphin is hiding at Chinon Castle, under attack by his court and afraid to fight. Even brave Dunois the Bastard cannot save Orleans; only a miracle can. Then it is the girl, suggests Polly, who is the miracle. Joan is sent for again and asked if she fully understands what she is proposing to do. Joan replies that the English are only men and have their own country and must be made to go back to it as God wants them to. And she will unite the divided French forces and drive out the English. The Squire, finding his interest growing, agrees that the troops, and even the Dauphin, might take courage from Joan's conviction. He orders her now to go to Chinon under escort and grants the soldier's dress she asks for. Joan runs happily offstage, Polly takes his leave, and the steward runs in to report that the hens have begun laying again!

Comment

Shaw establishes the Maid as direct, candid, strong in her belief and inspired by faith. Note, too, how much he tells us through dialogue of what we need in the way of background information. The scene is neatly rounded off with the **episode** of the steward and the eggs, as simple proof of Joan's divine mission, a small but telling miracle.

Scene Two

Setting

An antechamber in the throne room of the Dauphin's castle. Late afternoon, March, 1429.

The Archbishop and La Tremouille are contemptuously discussing the royal poverty, when Gilles de Rais, Bluebeard, enters. He cheerily relates news of the Maid's effect on the troops, in which he is confirmed by Captain La Hire, who now enters to report that Joan must be "an angel dressed as a soldier" and has made her difficult way here to Chinon. A page announces Charles, the Dauphin, who enters excitedly with a letter from de Baudricourt promising the Maid as a gift. He is bullied by his chamberlain and reproached by the Archbishop, both of whom want to refuse letting him see Joan. After some argument it is decided to follow a suggestion of Bluebeard: he will pretend to be the Dauphin, and when Joan arrives let them see if she can penetrate the disguise and find out the blood royal; if she can, it will be proof that she comes from God. Bluebeard and Charles leave the room to arrange for the impersonation, and the Archbishop and La Tremouille discuss the nature of miracles. A miracle, argues the Archbishop, is not simply a fraud, as La Tremouille would have it, but may be an innocent contrivance that serves to confirm the faith of the flock in the wisdom of the Church.

Now the curtains are drawn to reveal the full length of the throne room with the court assembled there. Joan's entrance in soldier's dress provokes laughter among the ladies. But all are quiet as the Maid approaches the circle of courtiers where Bluebeard poses as the Dauphin. Joan is not fooled. She pulls Charles from the crowd, kneels, and tells him that she has come to drive out the English and crown him King. She asks to speak with him alone, and the Archbishop, convinced now of her piety, says that she must be obeyed. To her Charles confesses his miserable insignificance and urges her to leave him be and not make him command. But Joan replies that she will put courage into him because God will have him King. She has come to get him to give up his kingdom to God, after which France will become holy, her divisions be healed, and the English beg to be allowed to go home in peace. She will dare all in God's name, she cries, and Charles must not betray her. Inspired now, the Dauphin recalls the court and announces he has just decided to give command of the army to Joan. Growling that he is commander, La Tremouille moves threateningly forward; but feeling Joan's hand on his shoulder, Charles snaps his fingers in the chamberlain's face. Joan then draws her sword and raises it to God, as do La Hire and the assembled knights. Joan falls to her knees in thanksgiving to God, followed by the others, except for the Archbishop, who gives a blessing, while La Tremouille fumes and curses.

Comment

The **exposition** of offstage events and the advancing action of the play are neatly dovetailed in this scene as we learn more about the condition of France. Note how economically Shaw dramatizes the corruption of the court and the paltriness of Charles. The scene between him and the Maid is a high point of the play. Like scene one, this scene moves to a theatrically effective **climax** in its last moments, with a smaller climax along the way in Joan's finding out of the true king. The ending of this scene should be kept in mind for comparison with the closing minutes of the Epilogue. As for the Archbishop's speech on miracles, it foreshadows some of the larger discussions of that subject which are to come.

Scene Three

Setting

South bank of the Loire, near Orleans.

Dunois the Bastard is pacing the river bank, imploring the west wind to spring up and replace the east wind that moves the pennon he has stuck on his lance to tell direction. He exchanges words with his pert page. A sentry's voice offstage halts Joan, and then she comes on in armor as the wind drops and the pennon sinks. She asks where the English are, and to Dunois' report that they are on all sides, replies that the French should cross the bridge and attack directly. Dunois chides her for wanting to do what the best military heads have said is impossible. But she wants to go up the ladder to the English fort with her sacred sword if Dunois will follow. He advises them to sail upstream and attack from the rear and then asks her to pray for a west wind. Joan starts off to find a church, when the page sneezes and calls out that the wind has changed! Dunois says God indeed has spoken and he will follow Joan the commander.

Comment

This short scene gives us still another miracle and shows the success Joan has in inspiring experienced soldiers like Dunois. At the close of the scene Joan begins to cry with joy at seeing the miracles the saints are working for her. Always she is acting in God's name, and the mixture of courage and faith in her is frequently touching. Her commonsensical opposition to the defeatism of the regular commanders is meant to be understood not simply as arrogance or self-sufficient pride but as the working of a rational nature impelled by belief in a divine errand.

Scene Four

Setting

A tent in the English camp.

The nobleman Warwick is discussing the recent French victories with his chaplain de Stogumber. A page announces Peter Cauchon, Bishop of Beauvais, whom Warwick has invited to confer with him about the Maid's advances and the inevitable crowning of Charles. Warwick introduces himself and his chaplain, then proceeds to ask Cauchon if there is any reasonable doubt that Joan is a sorceress, as de Stogumber vigorously asserts she is in view of her miraculous survivals in battle and her victories over the best English generals. Cauchon will concede only that she is an instrument of the Devil in his design to damn humanity. Further, she is a heretic, no a witch, and he, Cauchon, is concerned to save her soul. He is not, he says, concerned for either English interests or defeats, though Warwick says the Maid must be destroyed or the English cause will be lost.

Now Cauchon is moved to a long condemnation of Joan's presumption in bringing messages from God directly to the Dauphin without first consulting the Church and in acting as if she herself were the Church. He reviews the history of important heretics, those lapsed in faith, and scores impulsive mystics like Joan and Mahomet, who attend only to their voices and visions and ignore the authority of religious institutions. He vows to fight the growing influence of such people and to see Joan burned if she falls into his hands and will not submit completely to the rule of the Church. Warwick in turn proposes that a greater sin than her heresy is the threat she poses to the social structure of Europe. She is urging the kings, through Charles' example, to assume direct leadership of their countries and to dedicate them to God, bypassing the nobility and ruling as God's bailiff. Under this system the nobility will have to cede their lands to the King, who will then make a gift of them to God and earn the allegiance of the common people that was formerly granted to the individual baron or earl. Warwick decides that Joan's ideas about church and state are fundamentally identical since in each can be seen "the protest of the individual should against the interference of priest or peer between the private man and his God." He labels this thinking 'Protestantism," and Cauchon extends these remarks to apply them to another tendency that he can only call "nationalism." By filling the people with pride in their country and so dividing the kingdoms into nations, Joan is provoking another kind of heresy: the Church recognizes only one realm, the Kingdom of Christ, not separate entities called "nations." De Stogumber complains that the argument is becoming too subtle for him. He knows only that the Maid is a rebel against the Church, the Pope, Nature (by wearing man's clothing), and England. All agree' then, that she must be captured and her influence brought to an end.

Comment

This scene of discussion and debate is effective for several reasons. (1) Its **themes** are compactly organized in a progressive, forward-moving argument, and argumentation is the action of this scene. (2) Shaw assigns ideas to appropriate characters. Warwick is the representative of political and social feudalism; Cauchon, of the Church Universal (Catholic); and de Stogumber, also a churchman, of narrow-minded pride in his country, right or wrong. (3) The ideas are kept interesting by association with the characters and their positions. The blunt ferocity of de Stogumber is played off against the civilized skepticism of Warwick and the insistent clearmindedness of Cauchon. Accordingly, we feel a tension in the scene that keeps us alert not only to important ideas but also to character and motive. None of three men, then, is simply or crudely a mouthpiece for ideas; each has a distinctive dramatic life. We might note that scene four, coming in the center of the play, provides extensive interpretation of the first three scenes and perspective for viewing is to come.

Scene Five

Setting

Near the vestry in Rheims Cathedral.

Joan is kneeling before the altar following the coronation of Charles. Dunois enters to fetch her and bring her out to the people, but Joan tells him to let the King have all the glory. The Bastard notes that she has friends among the soldiers but not at court because the men she has showed up there as incompetent resent her. Then, Joan replies, she will go back to the farm once she has taken Paris. Dunois warns her that will not be an easy victory and she had better take care. Indeed, Joan admits, the world is too wicked for her. The only confidence she has now is the voices that keep telling her to be brave and go on.

The King enters with Bluebeard and La Hire, complaining of the weight of his robes and of the smell of the holy oil. He seems relieved and pleased to hear that Joan may be going home, which discourages the Maid. Still, she wants to take Paris with Dunois, a course that terrifies the King, who wants a treaty with the Burgundians and an end to fighting. The Archbishop, coming in now, tries to check Joan's impetuosity. He accuses her of disregarding God's will, for all her talk of faith, and says she invites tragic punishment for the sin humris (excessive daring or pride) well known to the Greeks. Again Joan pleads the authority of her voices and the fact of her triumphs. Dunois breaks in to remind her that God's miracles are not to be called on indefinitely; from now on good generalship and luck alone will win victories. And as for Joan, if she is ever captured and jailed, no one will risk his life to save her, not even he, Donois. The crown, says Joan, will come to her rescue then. No, contradicts Charles, he is not rich enough to ransom her. Will the Church aid her in that event? The Archbishop has only a warning of what she may expect at the hands of Cauchon. But Joan cannot believe they truly think her a witch, any more than she can understand, as the Archbishop now tells her, that her voices are echoes of her disobedient will. They have proved right all along, and earthly counsels wrong. She will be disowned by them all, warns the Archbishop-by the King, Dunois, the Church-as long as she sets up her judgment as superior to theirs. She stands alone, he says.

Now Joan turns on them and cries that she has always been alone, alone like France and like God Himself. And the loneliness of all three is their strength! She will dare in God's name until she dies. The love of the common people will repay her for the hatred of the court, and if she is burnt, she will go through the fire to their hearts forever. Then she goes out; Bluebeard remarking that she is quite impossible. Dunois says he will follow her but that if she is caught at Compiegne (near Paris) he will leave her to her doom. La Hire says he will follow her to Hell. The Archbishop admits she disturbs his judgment. And finally Charles speaks: "If only she would keep quiet, or go home!"

Comment

With this scene the play reaches a decisive turning point. By holding to the authority of her voices and refusing to take counsel, Joan has progressively cut herself off from sympathy, and from now on she will stand virtually alone. The speech on her aloneness is constructed on a base of the words "alone" or "loneliness" which recur to mark the **theme** of her isolation. Her position is characteristic of the hero or heroine of tragedy. Shaw seems to intend, by the Archbishop's reference to hubris, that Joan, though differently motivated, is of the stature of an Oedipus or Antigone in the ancient Greek tragedies. Her daring and her pride take the form of an unswerving belief in the voices and in her common sense of things. The voices for her are a kind of poetry she makes available to her followers in the form of good plain reason. She does not arrange miracles to impress them (recall the conversation of the Archbishop and La Tremouille in scene two); all she knows is that they occur, and at the same time she can give good military reasons for having won battles.

Scene Six

Setting

The Bishop's court at Rouen, 30 May, 1431.

Joan has been captured at Compiegne nine months before the opening of this scene, bought from the Burgundians by Warwick, then delivered to the ecclesiastical court for trial on charges of heresy. This is the morning of her seventh public trial. Before it begins Warwick converses with Cauchon, who introduces two other dignitaries, the chief inquisitor and Canon d'Estivet, promoter or prosecutor. Warwick is impatient at the delay in Joan's trial, but Cauchon reaffirms what he has said earlier, that this will be a fair trial uninfluenced by political expediency. And the inquisitor adds that Joan's examiners are all anxious to save her soul, though she is her own worst enemy, convicting herself every time she speaks. But Warwick is not satisfied and promises to act, if necessary, independently of the Church. He leaves as the assessors (judges) of the Bishop's court come in, headed by de Stogumber and a younger priest, Canon de Courcelles. Scribes and assessors take seats, but de Stogumber and Courcelles protest the reduction in the number of formal charges against Joan. The inquisitor replies that he has had them reduced in the interest of simplifying the proceedings.

And he insists that the main business is in trying Joan for heresy and not in attending to wild charges about her supposedly magical influence.

Another priest, Brother Martin Ladvenu, wishes to know if Joan's heresy is not merely a harmless form of simplicity, and his question brings a lengthy reply from the inquisitor. The burden of his speech is as follows. Heresy begins among people who are apparently lovable, pious, and say they reject the ways of the world in order to do God's work. But they and their followers set up their judgments ignorantly against that of the Church and interpret God's will by the light of their devilish inspiration which they believe divine. Joan is an example of this kind of heretic. In her, pride and humility go together, and the judges must not be too sympathetic to her. But they must avoid being cruel. The inquisitor mercifully sets about a fair examination of any charges and in a spirit of compassion attempts to save souls. Cauchon then speaks, urging the court to recognize the new and great heresy spreading everywhere, not just among the simpleminded, the heresy Warwick has called Protestantism and which threatens the whole structure of Catholic Christendom.

Joan is brought into the court now, wearing a page's costume and showing the strain of imprisonment. After some preliminaries, Cauchon asks her a most important question: Will she submit the judgment of her case to the heavenly inspired interpretation of the Church Militant? Joan says she will-and the judges lean forward expectantly-provided the Church does not command her to declare that her revelations and her orders were not from God or were Devil's work. Ladvenu tries to reason with her, to allay the impatience of Cauchon and the inquisitor. He wants her to say that she is subject to God's Church on earth, which she asserts she has never denied, though she puts

God Himself above the Pope, cardinals, and bishops and says repeatedly that He must be served first.

She insists upon the validity of her own judgment, and she hopes she is in a state of grace. Courcelles now is provoked to question her on minor matters, which throws the court into some disorder until the inquisitor restores calm. Joan then denies d'Estivet's charges that she has intercourse with evil spirits and she defends her dressing as a soldier. Her replies are sharp, so that more than once she has to be warned to answer in a way appropriate to the setting. But now her judges seem to give over questioning for the moment, as Ladvenu tells Joan to look around and see the executioner standing behind her, ready with the preparations for her burning in the event she is excommunicated and handed over to the English. Thinking her doom is near, Joan is filled with despair and fearfully accepts Ladvenu's and Cauchon's suggestions that the voices betrayed her into capture at Compiegne and are now leading her to the fire. She cries out that it must be true, she has been misled by devils - God will not ask her to go to the stake. The churchmen are relieved, and Ladvenu brings her a recantation of heresy to sign. De Stogumber rises in fury, accuses the court of treachery, and says the English will burn Joan in spite of ecclesiastical verdict.

Ladvenu reads aloud the document he wants Joan to sign. It is a confession to all the charges brought against her, followed by a statement of renunciation and an expression of gratitude to the Church and to the churchmen who have returned her to truth and grace. With Ladvenu guiding her hand, Joan writes her name and makes her mark by herself. Ladvenu thanks God, and the inquisitor pronounces Joan free from the danger of excommunication. But, he adds, for her presumption she must spend the rest of her days in solitary confinement, meditating and learning repentance. This is a sentence more terrifying to Joan than death. She snatches up the confession and tears it, crying that she was a fool to trust the court and that she cannot live shut away from life and nature and the sound of the church bells that bring her voices to her on the wind. Now she is attending to God's counsel, and the court's counsel is that of the Devil. This is what de Stogumber has been waiting for, and at his instructions the executioner rushes out to the marketplace to light his fire, while Ladvenu rebukes Joan's wickedness. She is God's child now, she declares, and not fit to live among them. Cauchon and the inquisitor pronounce her a lapsed heretic and excommunicate. They deliver her to the secular power and somewhat ambiguously urge moderation of the death sentence. Events move quickly. De Stogumber orders the soldiers to take Joan out to the fire. Ladvenu goes out to be at her side, and the glow of the bonfire can already be seen reddening the sky. Cauchon wants to hurry out to stop the burning, but the inquisitor checks him. He reminds Cauchon that the affair of the Maid is now in English hands. The Church has proceeded properly and a technical flaw or misstep by the English may someday prove useful to their opponents. But he admits it is terrible to see an ignorant innocent like Joan, who has not understood a word of what was said to her, crushed by the mighty forces of Church and Law.

Resigning themselves to the burning, they leave as Warwick enters. He calls for attendants and is surprised when de Stogumber staggers in and throws himself, sobbing, on the prisoner's stool. He blubbers that he had no notion of what he was doing and had never appreciated the reality of seeing someone burned. Thank God, he says, an English soldier gave Joan two sticks tied together when she asked for a cross. But he, de Stogumber, is forever damned. Ladvenu comes in to report that when he climbed the pyre to hold out a bishop's cross to

Joan, she urged him to think of his own safety, surely an action inspired by God. Warwick observes that the burning will have a bad effect on the people. De Stogumber rushes out to pray among her ashes, Warwick crying out to Ladvenu to follow him lest the chaplain do himself some harm. Warwick turns, and unexpectedly find the executioner in the room. He has come in to report that he has obeyed Warwick's orders to dispose of Joan's remains at the bottom of the river. Only her heart will not burn. But, he adds, Warwick has heard the last of her. Which makes Warwick smile wryly and wonder aloud if he has.

Comment

The **Climax** of the play was reached in scene five, in Joan's decision to stand alone, and scene six, which has climaxes of its own, is a resolving action that follows inevitably from it. In this scene all the issues of the play come together, all the conflicts of character and idea. In places it reminds one of scene four, but there is more variety of discussion here and the tension inherent in a court proceeding. Joan's faith and innocence, her simplicity and directness, shine through her testimony. Note the premonitions of the inquisitor. He knows that she is devout and not in league with the Devil, but he knows too that her very innocence, her failure intellectually to understand the import of the charges, will doom her. Note how Shaw distinguishes some of the churchmen, marking out the self-admiring legalism of d'Estivet, the shrillness of Courcelles, the gentle sanity of Ladvenu. It is their separate voices, played off against each other in the context of an ecclesiastical trial, that gives this scene historical and dramatic dimension. In a minor action, we see development in the character of de Stogumber. It is ironic that his ferocity turns back on him. Till now he has been partly a figure of fun, and the change in him to a broken, weeping, repentant man is striking. The high point of this scene is Joan's tearing up of the recantation she has signed. It marks the beginning of her passage to the stake and from there to immortality.

Epilogue

Setting

The bedroom of Charles VII (formerly the young Dauphin and now middle-aged). A windy night in June, 1456.

Reading in bed, Charles is disturbed by the sudden appearance at his side of Ladvenu, who has just come from a court rehabilitation where Joan has today been justified a declared innocent of the charges for which she was convicted twenty-five years earlier. Her judges have been declared full of malice and falsehood, and a great wrong has been set right. Charles cares only that it not be said he was crowned by a heretic and a witch, and observes that if Joan were to return she would be burned again within six months. Ladvenu, deploring the king's attitude, leaves.

The candles suddenly go out and a flash of summer lightning reveals the silhouette of a figure in the window, while the voice of Joan is heard telling Charles he is asleep and to rest easy. When she becomes visible she tells him he is dreaming but that she is dead nevertheless and wants to know what has been happening since she died. Charles tells her of her victory today and tries to convince her that she owes him thanks for bringing her justice. He is contradicted by Cauchon, who comes in as mysteriously as the others, and complains of the dishonor done him and the Church by the new verdict. He claims he was pure of heart at Joan's trial, faithful to his conception of the Church and its laws.

Now Joan asks what has happened to the English, and to answer her Dunois appears, saying the English are gone from France and his spirit is called not from death but from sleep. The clock strikes the third quarter to midnight as a new figure enters. It is that of a coarse English soldier, singing an improvised tune. He announces himself a soul from Hell who gets one day off a year for a good action. He - but Joan interrupts to speak for him - held up two sticks in the form of a cross to a poor girl at the stake. Now they hear a gentle knocking, and an old priest enters. It is de Stogumber, turned harmless, benevolent, astray in his wits from the shock of the sight he witnessed, and confessing that he warns his parishioners never to be cruel. His eyesight is bad too; he does not recognize Joan clearly. The executioner comes in too, reports that Joan's heart would not burn and that her spirit is alive everywhere. He is followed by Warwick, who congratulates Joan on her rehabilitation and insists there was nothing personal in her burning. Only political necessity dictates it, which, he admits, history has now found to be a political mistake, though Joan owes him her halo and Charles his crown.

A figure enters that causes them all to stare and then laugh. This is a clerical-looking gentleman of 1920, in frock coat and trousers. He reproves the laughter, announces serious business, and proceeds drily to read out the recent proclamation declaring the Venerable and Blessed Joan henceforth to be Saint Joan and ordering a memorial service to be celebrated on the anniversary of her death (signed at the Vatican May 16, 1920). De Stogumber asks for a statue of Joan to be placed in the Anglican cathedral at Winchester, and in a vision a statue is suddenly seen there and fades again. A second vision follows, of Joan on her horse, before Rheims Cathedral.

Now all kneel to Joan, whom Dunois calls the "soul of France." They offer her praise, one by one, in the name of the soldiers, the common people, the churchmen (the Archbishop and the inquisitor appear for this), the judges, the executioners, the foolish, the unpretending and the unheroic (like Charles). But Joan says she fears it when all men praise her. She is a saint and can work miracles. Shall she rise from the dead and come back to them? Consternation follows. They offer her apologies and excuses, all of which amount to saying No, they would rather have her dead. And they discreetly leave or steal away, except the gentleman of 1920, who bows formally and says he must leave to confer with Rome about the possibility of Joan's resurrection! Charles bids her goodnight and goes back to bed, agreeing with Dunois, who has just said they are none of them good enough for her yet. Joan is left with the soldier from Hell, but he too leaves as midnight strikes and continues to strike. The light of radiance descends on the Maid, alone on the stage, asking God when the world will be ready to receive his saints. "How long, O Lord, how long?"

Comment

The rehabilitation of Joan began a quarter century after her death and was finally accomplished by her election to sainthood in 1920. The epilogue finds the reversal of verdict both tragic and comic in its implications. It is tragic because Joan's death could have been avoided if men were more willing to welcome unsettling genius instead of martyring it ("The law of change is the law of God" is one of the topic headings of the preface). It is comic because men are inconsistent, even the wisest of them. The tone of the epilogue (all of which is a scene of fantasy), then, is serio-comic and most so in the climactic passage in which Joan asks her former allies and judges if they would like to see her return to them. Their frightened denial of her a second time may provoke laughter and a feeling of immense sadness. The last moment of the play should remind one of the close of scene two, when Joan knelt with upraised sword. But here she is without a weapon, talking to her God, alone. For all its overt statement of themes, *Saint Joan* as a drama reaches its profoundest meaning in the last image we have of the genius and the saint.

ANALYSIS OF SELECTED CHARACTERS

Joan

Her enemies are not only established institutions but her youth and her inexperience of the devious ways men reason. Her intelligence is too straightforward for the people she has to deal with and her position with respect to her voices and intuitions too uncompromising for them. The moment of her recantation is the only time of doubt in her mission, and her weakness then is understandably human as well as temporary. She expresses herself energetically and often colorfully. Like most of the characters embodying Shaw's idea of genius, she is a rationalist with the soul of a poet.

Cauchon

A sincere theologian, he represents the best lights of the Church on the problem Joan presents, the threat (and it is that to him) she poses of the individual, private conscience relying on itself for guidance rather than on the centuries-old, considered wisdom of the Church. But he is scrupulous in defending Joan against Warwick's political expediency and against the pettiness of the assessors at her trial Like the other churchmen, he is not an individualist and is proud of the traditions he stands for.

The Inquisitor

His considerations of Joan's case tend to be even more abstract than Cauchon's (though they are similar). He seems to speak not just for the moment but for all time. The sin of heresy strikes him to the soul. He appears to read in it man's helpless condition. His long speech on heresy shows his concern not only for the institutions he is expected to defend but for an erring humanity that needs correction and guiding back to the true path that leads to salvation.

Warwick

He is a nobleman to the end, courteous, proud, witty, believing in the traditions of his class and holding little hope for most people outside of it. He is keenly aware of all political motivations, and he tries subtly and openly to maneuver the outcome of Joan's trial in the direction of English interests. Superficially he may appear to be a gentleman and something of a dandy, but he is a shrewd tactician who will use logic and reason only up to a point and a show of force after.

De Stogumber

To contrast him with Warwick, one sees his limitations immediately. There is no subtlety about this man. He defends Englishmen against foreigners on any occasion and is intolerant of any suggestion that the English are not in every way superior to their adversaries. He is often the butt of jokes (scene four) for his blunt and narrow patriotism, but they leave him unmoved. Only Joans' burning, the power of whose effect on him he had not considered, makes any change in him.

The Dauphin

He is much like a spoiled child, perverse and changeable. He is intelligent, we should note, and weak. When we first see him, he is not a mover of men primarily because he has no confidence in himself as a Prince or a man. In the epilogue, he says he has turned out to be not a bad leader after all and has more effective in his way than all the important people who condemned the Maid. But he is never loyal to her. She makes him uncomfortable and he wants her out of the way.

GEORGE BERNARD SHAW

CANDIDA

CHARACTERS

Candida Morell

Thirty-three, wife of Reverend Morell.

James Morell

Forty, a vigorous Christian Socialist Clergyman.

Eugene Marchbanks

Eighteen, an aristocratic poet and idealist, in love with Candida.

Mr. Burgess

Candida's father, a businessman.

Proserpine Garnett

Thirty, Morell's adoring secretary.

Alexander Mill

A recent graduate of Oxford, a curate and assistant to Morell.

SETTING

Morell's parsonage in a poor district of London.

The action of the play occupies a morning, afternoon, and evening of a day in 1894. The Reverend Morell, a busy, energetic, well-liked minister, discovers that the young man he has befriended, Eugene Marchbanks, is in love with his attractive wife Candida. At first Morell is inclined to make light of Marchbanks' highly romantic and poetic professions of love and of his charges that the clergyman does not appreciate her, whereas he, the poet, does and is the proper mate for her. But soon Morell sees that Marchbanks is serious and reports the news to Candida. She has known all along. She understands both men in their strength and their weakness and loves them both. But, she says, at the **climax**, she will give herself to the weaker of the two. Marchbanks knows who that is. It is Morell, who needs his wife and the mother of his children. And so Marchbanks, with "a secret in his heart," that he can sustain himself by his visions of the ideal, and does not need Candida, leaves.

Comment

This is a very neatly constructed play, with climaxes well placed to maintain suspense. The scene in which Marchbanks and Morell bid for Candida is highly skillful. Candida is a woman of immense charm, conventional, and no homebreaker. She understand and manages her husband for his own good and yet is capable of attracting the young poet. But in the end she cannot keep him. He sees family that he can stand alone, that he has what Morell does not, the strength to dream and to search for the ideal. He is the end a more practical man than the enthusiastic socialist clergyman with all his projects of reform and uplift. Candida is considered one of the best female parts in the Shavian repertory. She is the ideal to all men, wise, dignified, feminine maternal. Marchbanks grows up in the course of the play, and beyond the love of woman, but we must appreciate her magnetism all the same. The role of Marchbanks is difficult and problematic. His effusiveness is callow and often seems like a caricature of the poet speaking. But there is strength in the characterization, and the actor must find it in Marchbanks' unconventional view of things. Indeed it may be argued that Marchbanks is the center character of this play.

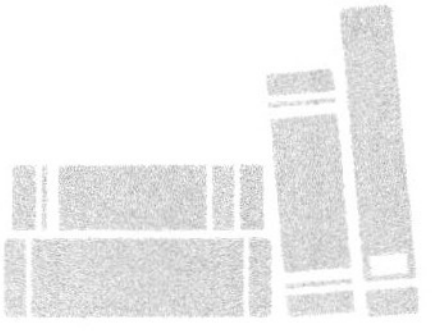

GEORGE BERNARD SHAW

THE DEVIL'S DISCIPLE

CHARACTERS

Richard Dudgeon

A young man of unconventional views.

Mrs. Dudgeon

His mother, stern and hard-hearted.

Christy

The younger son, crass and stupid.

Essie

A pretty orphan of sixteen, brought up by Mrs. Dudgeon.

William Dudgeon

A Dudgeon uncle, a poor relation.

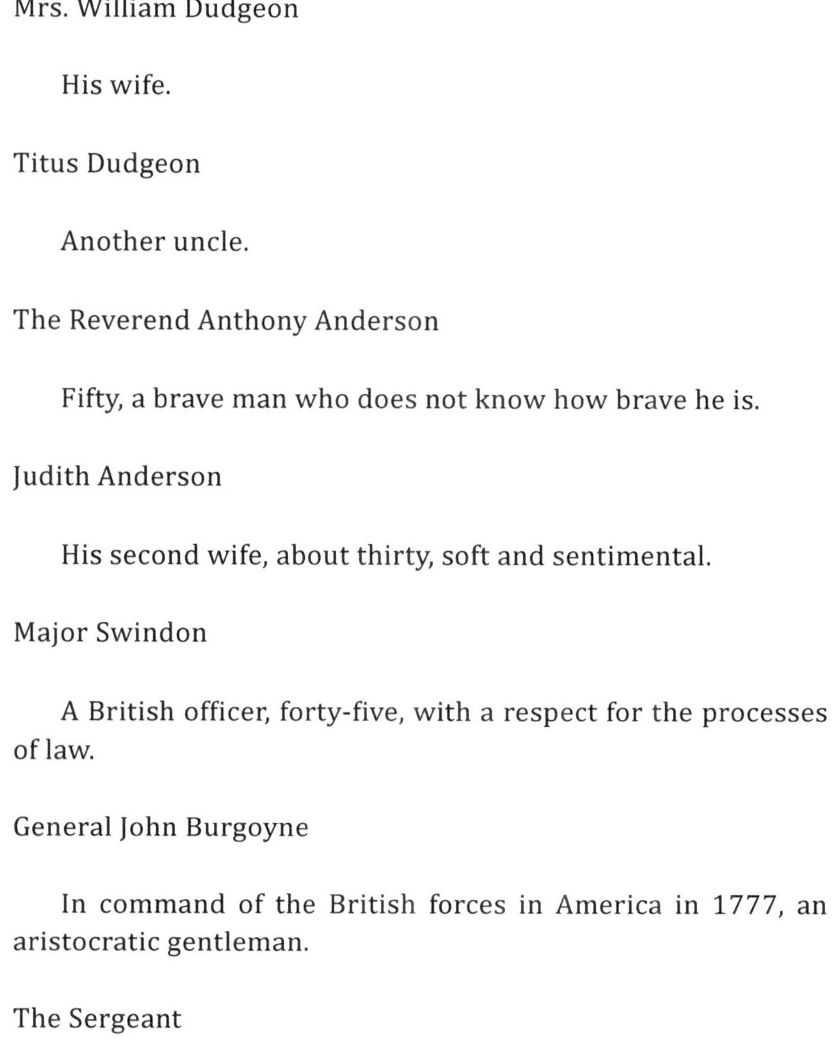

Mrs. William Dudgeon

His wife.

Titus Dudgeon

Another uncle.

The Reverend Anthony Anderson

Fifty, a brave man who does not know how brave he is.

Judith Anderson

His second wife, about thirty, soft and sentimental.

Major Swindon

A British officer, forty-five, with a respect for the processes of law.

General John Burgoyne

In command of the British forces in America in 1777, an aristocratic gentleman.

The Sergeant

A British soldier.

Mr. Brudenell

A Chaplain of the British army.

Lawyer Hawkins

The Dudgeon family lawyer.

British And German Officers, Townspeople, A Town Beadle.

SETTING

Westerbridge, New Hampshire, 1777.

During the troubled times of the American Revolution, Richard Dudgeon arrives home to learn that his father has died suddenly and left everything to him on condition that Richard look after Essie, his reprobate uncle's natural child. Richard is glad to rescue her from the bigoted Mrs. Dudgeon, a woman intensely conscious of sin, for whom Richard is a lost soul, though he voluntarily regards himself as the Devil's disciple, a fighter against the harsh, narrow Puritan morality of his mother. In the second act Richard is mistaken for the Reverend Anderson by the British and condemned to be hanged as a warning to the rebellious community. Richard refuses to allow the minister's wife to tell the truth and stands court martial before General Burgoyne. But she cannot contain herself and speaks out. Still the trial goes against the hostage, despite Richard's witty parrying with the relaxed and civilized Burgoyne. At the moment of execution the Reverend Anderson rides in with negotiations for the British to evacuate Westerbridge. The minister has found his true vocation as a man of action, and the Devil's disciple, Richard, is now released, free to follow his own natural bent toward sacrifice and, if need be, martyrdom.

Comment

Shaw has taken the standard apparatus of period melodrama - heroic men, dangerous situations, a trial and a last minute rescue from the gallows - and converted it to higher purposes than mindless entertainment. Dudgeon is one of the first of his heroes of the Devil's party; that is, a man who flouts **convention** in order to free himself and others from outworn and spurious obligations, who risks his life because it is in his nature to put a hard test on himself. Dudgeon rejects the forbidding ethic his mother preaches in favor of his own more generous one, and in a reversal of roles, helps the minister to find a mission. The play is perhaps most notable for the trial scene, wherein the firmness of Richard's belief meets the skeptical questioning of the elegant General Burgoyne, a matching of the new revolutionary man (Dudgeon) with the representative of the established order (Burgoyne).

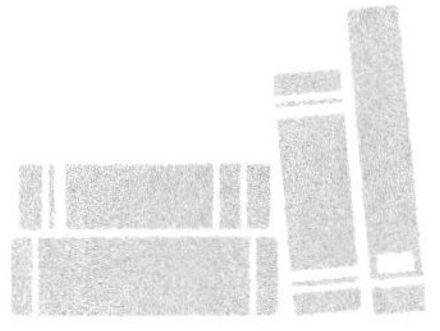

GEORGE BERNARD SHAW

THE MAN OF DESTINY

CHARACTERS

Napoleon Bonaparte

Twenty-seven years old.

The Lady

A clever, bewitching, extremely feminine young woman.

The Lieutenant

A young French officer, easily imposed upon.

Giuseppe

The talkative, shrewd innkeeper.

SETTING

The main room of an Italian inn, May, 1796.

In this one-act play, the young Napoleon has just experienced victory in his Italian campaign and is waiting at an inn for military dispatches to be brought him. The Lieutenant who is supposed to bring them confesses he unwittingly allowed them to be stolen by a youth he met on his way. Eventually this "youth" turns out to be a lady upstairs at the inn, who was in disguise and desperate, she tells Napoleon, to retrieve from among those dispatches a letter involving the honor of a woman. The play is taken up with the duel of wits and sexual attraction between the lady and the young Bonaparte. At the end each recognizes the other as an equal and together they burn the incriminating letter.

Comment

This short play is an essay in historical biography that may be seen as anticipating the more ambitious and important *Caesar and Cleopatra* (1898). Napoleon here is at the beginning of his career and is not the emperor of legend. He is depicted as a man who lives without the illusions and **conventions** that shackle the behavior of most men, who works hard, is unscrupulous when necessary, and is capable of strong, simple actions which will make him master of his destiny. The lady recognizes these qualities and her cleverness is a match for his. The play makes use of some of the **conventions** of romantic melodrama (compare *Arms and the Man*) like disguise and the intrigue of secret dispatches. A high point of the play is the description by Napoleon of the character and morality of the English, a passage that is satirical in intent and may be compared with some of the speeches of Tanner in *Man and Superman* or the characterization of Britannus, the respectable Briton, in *Caesar and Cleopatra*. Altogether *The Man of Destiny* is a slight but not trivial play.

GEORGE BERNARD SHAW

MISALLIANCE

CHARACTERS

John Tarleton

A middle-aged underwear manufacturer, expansive and genial.

Hypatia

His attractive daughter.

Johnny

His son, an ordinary young businessman.

Mrs. Tarleton

His shrewd and agreeable wife.

Bentley Summerhays

A delicate young man.

Lord Summerhays

His father, formerly of the Colonial service.

Joey Percival

A young aviator, pursued by Hypatia.

Lina Szczepanowska

A high-spirited Polish aviatrix and acrobat.

Julius Baker (Gunner)

A clerk seeking vengeance.

SETTING

The Tarleton house in the country.

The action of the play is continuous, undivided, and a little unusual in that large parts of it are taken up with discussion and debate of topics interesting to the characters and especially to John Tarleton, a great reader and talker who amuses and challenges his family by his ideas. He has them and their guests, the Summerhays, father and son, talking on and on, when an airplane crashes into the greenhouse and brings adventure. This adventure arrives in the form of Joey Percival, whom Hypatia sets her cap for, and of the fascinating acrobat Lina Szczepanowska whose courage and beauty immediately captivate all the men. As though things are not lively enough now, Gunner Baker appears from town, a downtrodden little clerk looking to punish the man who ruined his mother long ago, (this man being Tarleton). The complications are finally worked out after much discussion: Hypatia gets her Joey, Lina takes Bentley away with her to make a man of him, and Gunner is consoled by Mrs. Tarleton - so that finally old Tarleton has to admit there is nothing left to talk about. And the play ends.

Comment

The preface contains a compact discussion of the play's subject, the relations of parents and children. The play itself is freewheeling in its treatment of its **theme**, sometimes appearing to be digressive and even irrelevant. One critic, Eric Bentley, has termed this play "disquisitory," that is, on the order of a discourse or inquiry into a subject. All the same, it is not undramatic; in fact, it is one of the most attractive of Shaw's plays and is coming increasingly into public favor. Much of the overt debate and speech-making is impressive and amusing and there is enough comic, even farcical invention to keep the play moving. The spirit of the play is happy, though shot through
moving. The spirit of the play is happy, though shot through with traces of wistful seriousness that sometimes turns into pathos.

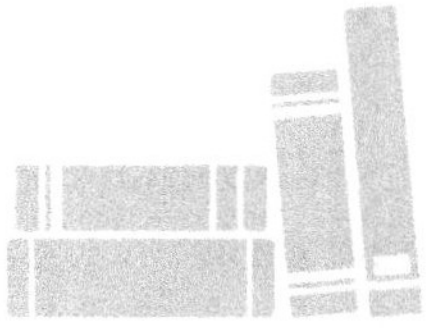

GEORGE BERNARD SHAW

ANDROCLES AND THE LION

INTRODUCTION: A FABLE PLAY (1911-1912)

CHARACTERS

Androcles

A Greek tailor of no determinable age.

Megaera

His shrewish wife.

The Lion

A likeable beast.

Lavinia

A young Christian woman.

The Captain

A handsome Roman officer.

Caesar

Emperor of Rome (but not Julius Caesar).

Lentulus

Fashionable Romans.

Metellus

Fashionable Romans.

Spintho

Fashionable Romans.

Ferrovius

A Christian convert of great strength, brother of Lavinia.

Centurion

A kind of army Sergeant.

Editor

In charge of the gladiatorial games.

Soldiers, Christian, Gladiators, Attendants, Menagerie-Keeper, Call Boy

SETTING

Rome during the era of Christian persecution.

This play follows the outlines of the ancient fable of the slave who drew the thorn from the lion's paw and was later recognized and saved by the lion in the Coliseum. Shaw includes other actions: the love of the Roman captain for the Christian Lavinia whose religious sincerity he finds compelling and the repentance of the physically powerful Ferrovius, who has foresworn violence in the best Christian manner until he is faced with six of the Emperor's gladiators and cannot resist saving his life at the expense of theirs. The play closes with the joyous meeting of Androcles and the playful lion before the eyes of the astonished Romans. These two so delight everyone that the Emperor pardons all the Christian, ordering his soldiers, to become Christians since they fight so well; Ferrovius accepts a place in the Emperor's guard; Lavinia promises to let the Captain come and converse with her; and Androcles goes off with the lion.

Comment

Shaw has written a very long preface to this short play in which he discusses Christianity, and he has added some pages following the play to point up the **themes** of *Androcles and the Lion*. It is essentially a play about religious belief. The Romans are obeying the dictates of an outworn religion, whereas the Christians sustain themselves with the ideal of a new creed. But the opposition is not simple. Lavinia is beautifully intelligent in her worship, just as Ferrovius is blunt and unimaginative in his. It takes a crisis to show him that he is a fighter at heart who must live by that vocation until the Christian god truly comes to be. And Lavinia lives by the ideal of God because God is the only real thing, she argues, worth dying for. For all its seriousness, the play is cast as a comic fable and makes much of the scenes with the lion, most notably the last one, in which Androcles and the lion dance in the arena.

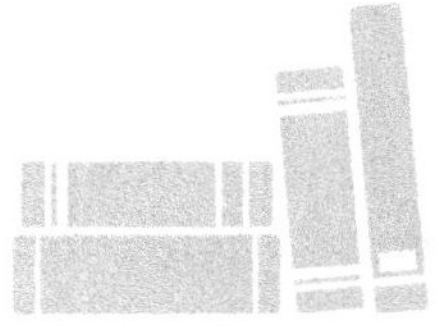

GEORGE BERNARD SHAW

HEARTBREAK HOUSE

INTRODUCTION: A FANTASIA IN THE RUSSIAN MANNER ON ENGLISH THEMES (1913-1916)

CHARACTERS

Captain Shotover

A disillusioned man of eighty.

Hesione Hushabye

One of his two daughters, a siren of a woman, forty-four.

Lady Utterwood

The other daughter, forty-two, wife of a Colonial administrator.

Ellie Dunn

A pretty girl with much to learn about life.

Mazzini Dunn

Her idealistic father.

Boss Mangan

A middle-aged capitalist Hector Hushabye A romantic man of fifty.

Randall Utterwood

An agreeable idler.

Nurse Guinness

An exasperated servant.

The Burglar

A pathetic intruder.

SETTING

Captain Shotover's house in Sussex "on a fine evening at the end of September."

This complexly symbolical and mysterious play brings all of its characters together in the house of old Captain Shotover, a retired seaman and inventor, who runs his house like a ship and who is disillusioned with himself and his family and indeed with mankind (note the exhaustion symbolized in his name). The main action has to do with the education of the innocent Ellie Dunn in the ways of a group of people who are desperately frivolous and played out (the Hushabyes and Utterwoods); in the illusions of power fostered by her fiance, Boss Mangan, a predatory capitalist who is not as formidable as everyone supposes; and in the true purposes of life by the ancient, half-mad Captain to whom she offers her love in exchange for his broken wisdom. There is some digression in the intrusion of a burglar with a scheme for attracting sympathy and money from his victims, after which the play returns to its main issues. In the last act, the inhabitants of Heartbreak House, Ellie's name for this place of vain hopes and agonizing delusions, try to work out their complicated relations. They are interrupted by a threatening enemy airplane (it is wartime) that drops a bomb and destroys Mangan and the burglar, the two practical men of business. The Captain sees it as a judgment of God on the society he is so bitterly alienated from, while Mrs. Hushabye is excited by the sounds in the sky, and Ellie, in the last line, hopes too that the planes will come again the next night.

Comment

By "fantasia" Shaw indicates a free play of imagination over his themes without too much regard for dramatic form. In this, *Heartbreak House* is another "disquisitory" drama, its subject, according to the preface, "cultured, leisured Europe before the war." The "Russian manner" of the title refers to some plays of the Russian dramatist, Anton Chekhov (1860-1904), whom Shaw greatly admired, that also examine the well-to-do, idle, introspective occupants of a Russian Heartbreak House. These characters have no visible purpose in living, and in Shaw's play the heartbreaking tragedy is that these are the very people who make up the governing classes and are, according to Shotover, bringing the whole ship of democracy on the rocks. The Captain is very often seen to stand for the author himself, and in some productions the actor has made himself up to look like the bearded and aged Bernard Shaw (note, however, Shaw was not eighty in 1913). He offers little consolation to youth, represented by Ellie, who wants the ideal he proposes; "Life with a blessing!" But that does not seem to be attainable in this sad, half allegorical play.

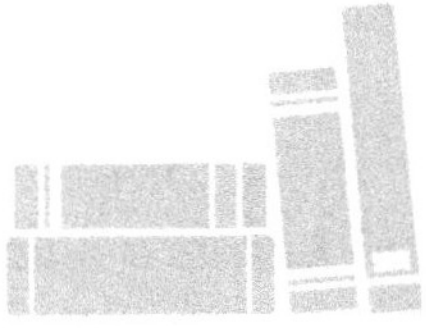

ESSAY QUESTIONS AND ANSWERS

ARMS AND THE MAN

Question: What may one say about the construction of this play?

Answer: *Arms and the Man* is a very well-constructed play and an excellent example of Shaw's control of dramatic technique. The play is neat, compact, and logical. All the incidents fit economically together and there are no loose ends in the plotting (that is, in the arrangement and patterning of the play's events). In the plays of this early period, Shaw is given to this kind of construction; it is not always welcomed today and seems to some critics like old-fashioned carpentering. There is nothing discursive in the play, no motion wasted, as there frequently is in some of the later works (so dissatisfying a second group of critics). Shaw here knows the craft of playwriting, especially the techniques of suspense, surprise, reversal, and above all, the clever complication of events followed by the clear unraveling and resolution of the various actions of the play.

Question: What relation, if any, has the Louka-Nicola action to the rest of the play?

Answer: The two servants represent a variation on the key **theme** of the play: reality versus romance. Nicola is the sensible man who recommends caution and prudence to the headstrong Louka. It is his sense of the way things are with servants and masters, of that reality, that has made him a trusted servant of the Petkoffs. She wants the romance of rising above her station and is not content with the life of a servant. Still, she sees that he is right in what he says and confesses he takes the heart out of her. That she finally wins Sergius is a triumph to be had only in plays, but it confirms her belief in her daydream. Romance and reality are opposed in the Bluntschli-Raina-Sergius action. Raina learns that there are other kinds of heroes than the ones she favors in fiction, Bluntschli being far from her storybook ideal. And Sergius learns that war is hell and love a fraud when conducted in the extravagant way he is so fond of. He is disillusioned and it takes the good sense of Bluntschli and the courage of Louka to cheer him up by the end of the play. The opposition of reality to romance, then, is played out on these two levels of the action. And as we can see from Bluntschli's admission of the romance in his own practical soul, the opposition is not clear; there remains some ambiguity about this opposition, and the author's witty recognition of it is one of the sources of our pleasure in this play.

CAESAR AND CLEOPATRA

Question: How close to history is *Caesar and Cleopatra*? What is Shaw's intention in this history play?

Answer: This is one of a number of Shaw's excursions into historical interpretation. History and biography provided his lively intelligence with material for speculation about men and their motives. On a number of occasions it seems to have provided him with the stimulus for writing plays; in this outline alone, consider the plays under discussion, *The Devil's Disciple* (Burgoyne is an actual personage), *The Man of Destiny*, and *Saint*

Joan. As a literal record of events Shaw's history plays have no value, for he is very free in his interpretation of people and events and not at all concerned with factual chronicling of the ordinary kind. In *Caesar and Cleopatra*, Shaw has allowed his imagination to work at liberty over some of the most renowned occurrences of ancient history. His attitude is that of a dramatist or creative historian trying to see a pattern in a personality or event. Like Shakespeare, Shaw creates his own history within the confines of some accepted happenings and dates. It is interesting in this respect to consider the view of history Shaw assigns Caesar in the play. For Caesar history seems to be a shameful record of man's folly and crime. It has to be lived down, not cherished, atoned for and made good if it is not to repeat itself in an endless succession of uncivilized actions.

Question: What is the relationship of Caesar and Cleopatra?

Answer: Their relationship is largely that of pupil and teacher. Caesar tries to educate Cleopatra, to teach her the lessons he has had to learn the hard way. She is educable but not reliable. She seems to understand what he tells her about the folly of human treachery and political vindictiveness. But in a crisis she backslides and orders the savage murder of Pothinus. Caesar has come to acknowledge his own crime, his share in the murder of Pompey, and regrets it. As a political realist he is not of the ordinary kind: His actions are consistently performed in the light of an ideal he has about making the world a more reasonable place. He tries to teach Cleopatra that idealism of his kind is the best **realism** in the end. Their relationship is important too for an appreciation of the structure of the play. All of the scenes are moments in her education by a man of greatness, and the dramatic tensions throughout are realized in the struggle of the enlightened teacher to make his lessons understandable to all of those (not just Cleopatra) about him.

Consider how many characters are educated by Caesar in one way or another, and the truth of this will be apparent.

MAN AND SUPERMAN

Question: Is it possible to appreciate *Man and Superman* fully without the Philosophy?

Answer: The Comedy makes a complete play with all the dramatic situations and motives satisfactorily worked out. In his voluble fashion, Tanner touches upon and often explores all the **themes** of the Dialogue in Hell, as the Philosophy is sometimes called. However, it may be argued that one **theme** does not find its full expression in the Comedy, for all its brilliance, and that is the **theme** of the Superman. It is partly the purpose of the Philosophy to demonstrate the need for the Superman. The Devil argues that man is totally corrupt, Juan the hero has not been brave enough yet to live up to his best impulses. What is needed is the Superman, the superior being, the philosophic man with idealism to sustain him and the sense of hard obligation to keep him striving for a better world. A race of Supermen would be best of all. To begin their creation Ann in the Comedy is willing to give herself to painful childbirth and Tanner finally to give up his freedom to the irresistible demands of the Life Force. One needs the dialogue, then, to appreciate the momentousness of the struggle between Tanner and Ann. It's idealism informs the whole play and indeed most of Shaw's work. All the great figures of his plays are philosophic men (and women) with a vision of a better humanity, a future of Supermen. In the early plays, the philosophic man is clearing the ground for the position the later heroes take. Richard in *The Devil's Disciple* prefigures Tanner, and even Marchbanks in *Candida*, with the secret in his heart, has a little of the moral passion and the philosophic vision. It is more completely realized in Caesar, in Undershaft, in Tanner, of course, and in *Saint Joan*. These characters are considered in their plays as clever, perverse, or destructive. Others will not take Tanner seriously and think him a pleasant crank. Caesar has the admiration of all-provided he keeps the upper hand. But Joan threatens too many important institutions. These heroic characters live without illusions as does Napoleon in *The Man of Destiny*, who is not a philosophic man though he shares some of his traits. That is the first prerequisite for seeing clearly. Bluntschli is like that, also Richard. Both see through the self-deceptions by which the people around them live. When this character is given a purpose that challenges his society importantly, he becomes the genius figure of the major plays.

MAJOR BARBARA

Question: What is the significance of Bill Walker's taunting of Barbara with his "What price salvation now?" in Act Two?

Answer: His question (or his taunt) points up Barbara's dilemma: Shall she take Undershaft's money and compromise, as she thinks, the Army's integrity? Or shall she accept the future rewards of salvation and lose the usefulness of tainted money? She has tried to save Walker by her earnestness, and now her father's gift threatens to undo all her work. Walker's question sneers at the piety of the Army by pointing out that piety can be bought. It is a crisis for Barbara and is the **climax** of the play, followed by her giving up of her rank. It will take another act and the forceful arguments of Undershaft (note the name, with its suggestions of getting under one's guard with a telling shaft) to convince her that she and her father are not on opposing sides. They both want to see men saved, but their conceptions of salvation differ (until the third act). Thereafter they agree that the Kingdom of God will be realized only after man's body has been saved.

Question: Comment on the Faith of the Armorer in Act III.

Answer: Undershaft's recitation of the Armorer's creed is one of the most impressive moments in the play. It is not a simple rationalization of a wicked munitioner's practice. It is an article of faith, with religious and mystical overtones. Its parts are worth examining separately because they concentrate much of the meaning of the play. Undershaft is typical of the artist-philosophers in Shaw's plays and is one in the tribe of philosophic men. All of these men have a religion they have fashioned for themselves out of reason added to intuition. They express themselves eloquently when challenged. Note the impressive rhetoric of Undershaft's main arguments about poverty, comparing it with some speeches of Juan or Caesar. In all of these, the sentences are composed like an orator's speech, to have the maximum effect on an audience. Their logic is sometimes overwhelming, and they are intense and passionate. Read over, for example, Caesar's address to the Sphinx or Juan's on the frailties of mankind.

PYGMALION

Question: Does this play have any relation to the other major plays?

Answer: *Pygmalion* seems to some readers unlike other Shaw plays they are familiar with. Shaw does not seem so much concerned in it with his favorite themes. This play they find lighter than *Caesar and Cleopatra* or *Man and Superman* for example. But on closer examination it will be seen that *Pygmalion* does share some of Shaw's preoccupations. It is solidly constructed on the base of a leading Shavian idea: The differences between one man and another are social, not natural, differences. Eliza has as much intelligence as her betters, but it is hidden by the poverty into which she was born and that keeps her in subjection. Under training she reveals her natural capacity. She is quick to learn and has a mind and spirit of her own. In polite society she can pass as a duchess. Shaw, of course, may be having a joke at the expense of popular romantic notions of duchesses. He may be saying that it is not so hard to learn to be a duchess once you understand that a duchess is not as elevated as she appears. The Sequel brings the play firmly into the context of the major Shavian ideas, if not completely of the major plays. The spirit of this comedy is alien to the passionate version of *Caesar and Cleopatra*, but note the similarity: Caesar and Higgins are both educators. Higgins is much like John Tanner, bun *Pygmalion* does not pretend to have the intellectual scope of *Man and Superman*. *Pygmalion* is perhaps close in feeling to the Comedy parts of that play or to a simpler play like *Arms and the Man*, which is anti-romantic. *Pygmalion* is called a "romance," and proves, like all Shavian romances, to be the reverse of what is promises. It is, if one likes, a fairy story with a difference.

Question: Is the Doolittle action important to *Pygmalion*?

Answer: The rise of Alfred Doolittle from dustman to moral reformer underlines Shaw's **theme**. Doolittle makes the leap from one social class to a higher one almost by accident. His native wit gets him by, just as Eliza's intelligence and charm make her successful. His origins then go unquestioned as Doolittle dazzles his hearers with his unconventional morality. In short, Doolittle embodies the second joke the play makes about class relations: how either by design or by accident one can surmount the class barriers that have always seemed so insurmountable. Note, by the way, how much like Higgins Doolittle is. He speaks his mind and refuses to have his life guided by middle-class standards of respectability. This is why Higgins finds him so interesting. It may be argued that in Act Five we have too much of Doolittle, that his rise to eminence does not fit well with the rest of the play. It is a romance, too, like Eliza's transformation, but it is played as a farce in a comedy that makes most of its points in a non-farcical way. For all the wittiness of his speeches, there is something gratuitous, something slightly forced, about the dramatic invention that brings Doolittle to the attention of an American millionaire.

SAINT JOAN

Question: How accurate is Shaw's portrait of Joan and her times?

Answer: They are as accurate as Shaw could make it from the biographies and histories he read. But the word "accurate" is questionable here, since accuracy is not a criterion that Shaw is necessarily concerned with. He is "accurate" enough about events, about names and dates, but his portrayal of Joan rests upon his interpretation of her story. His play makes such an interpretation, showing Joan as a Shavian genius figure-a natural genius not a saint in woman's clothing-who comes to grief because the world is not yet ready for her. Shaw has depicted this figure before in one way and another: Bluntschli, Caesar, Dudgeon, Tanner-all prefigure Joan. Bluntschli is a simple version of the clever man who thinks for himself; Joan is a more complex version of the same figure taken up almost 30 years later. Accuracy of a literal kind, then, is irrelevant here. But it is important to note that Shaw tries for objectivity. He says in the preface that his play has no heroes and villains in the ordinary sense, and it does not. He tries to see the Church's view of things as much as he does Joan's. He does not make the

Church unsympathetic. He dramatizes the conflict of two forces, the Church's authoritarianism with Joan's individualism, of the medieval social order with the new "Protestantism" in every sphere of life.

Question: What is the purpose of the Epilogue to *Saint Joan*?

Answer: The Epilogue comments on all that has come before it. The issues of the play and the central conflicts are clear as early as scene four, and the tragic martyrdom of the Maid is completed after the trial. The play might have ended with scene six and the closing line of Warwick that looks ahead to Joan's disturbing immortality ("The last of her? Hm! I wonder!"). But the Epilogue brings everything into the perspective of modern times by taking account of Joan's rehabilitation. The Epilogue is unlike the rest of the play: It is fantasy, whereas the prevailing mode of *Saint Joan* might be called historical **realism**. And the Epilogue makes the point of the play. The spectator may be inclined to write down Joan's persecution to the superstition and ignorance vulgarly associated with the Middle Ages. Shaw will not let him off so easily. Joan is a genius figure and is no more assured of an easy reception in our age than she was in her own. She is too unsettling, makes everyone uncomfortable. Nobody wants her to come back to life, despite her canonization. The Gentleman of 1920 is flustered by her suggestion that she can return to earth, and has to get advice from Rome. Joan's contemporaries know how dangerous she was and is to their complacency and peace of mind; and their attitude, Shaw proposes, is timeless. The Epilogue, then, faces the ironic disparity between Joan's sainthood and her second rejection by men. Geniuses are better dead. Shaw treats all of this comically, but the comedy has sadness beneath it. Shaw was nearly seventy when he wrote *Saint Joan*. He might well have begun to despair of the earth's ever being ready (in the Maid's closing words) to receive its saints.

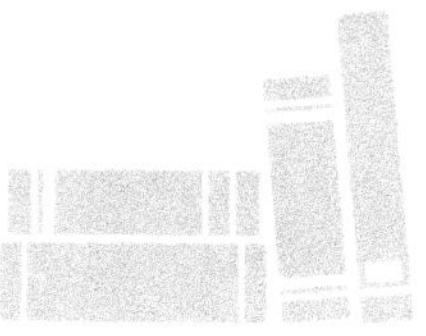

BIBLIOGRAPHY AND GUIDE TO FURTHER RESEARCH

ON MODERN DRAMA IN ENGLAND

Bentley, Eric, *The Playwright as Thinker*, N. Y., 1946; revised 1955.

Downer, Alan S., *The British Drama*, N. Y., 1950.

Nicoll, Allardyce, *British Drama*, London, 1947, revised.

Shaw, G. B., *Our Theatres in the Nineties*, 3 vols., London, 1931.

Trewin, J. C., *The Theatre Since 1900*, London, 1951.

ON GEORGE BERNARD SHAW

Bentley, Eric, *Bernard Shaw*, N. Y., 1947; amended 1957 as *Bernard Shaw, 1856-1950*.

Ervine, St. John, *Bernard Shaw, His Life, Works and Friends*, N. Y., 1956.

Henderson, Archibald, *Bernard Shaw: Man of the Century*, N. Y., 1956.

Irvine, William, *The Universe of G. B. S.*, N. Y., 1959.

Kaye, Julian B., *Bernard Shaw and the Nineteenth-Century Tradition,* Norman, Oklahoma, 1958.

Kronenberger, Louis (Ed.), *George Bernard Shaw. A Critical Survey,* Cleveland and N. Y., 1953.

Mander, Raymond, and Joe Mitcheson, *The Theatrical Companion to Shaw: A Pictorial Record of the First Performances of the Plays of G.B.S., with Synopses, Casts and Detailed Notes,* N. Y., 1955.

Nethercot, A. H., *Men and Supermen: The Shavian Portrait Gallery,* Cambridge, Mass., 1954.

Purdom, C. B., *A Guide to the Plays of Bernard Shaw,* London, 1963.

Rattray, R. F., *Bernard Shaw: A Chronicle,* London, 1951.

BOOKS ABOUT SHAW BIOGRAPHY

Ervine, St. John, *Bernard Shaw: His Life, Work and Friends,* New York: William Morrow and Company, 1956. The author, an Irish playwright and friend of Shaw, is sympathetic to Shaw as a person but criticizes his ideas at great length. The personal details about Shaw's life are much more interesting than the criticism.

Henderson, Archibald, *George Bernard Shaw: Man of the Century,* New York: Appleton-Century-Crofts, 1956. The most complete biography of Shaw.

Pearson, Hesketh, *G. B. S., A Full-Length Portrait,* New York and London: Harper and Brothers, 1942. Contains an excellent selection from Shaw's correspondence.

BOOKS ABOUT SHAW BIOGRAPHY

Ervine, St. John, *Bernard Shaw: His Life, Work and Friends*, New York: William Morrow and Company, 1956. The author, an Irish playwright and friend of Shaw, is sympathetic to Shaw as a person but criticizes his ideas at great length. The personal details about Shaw's life are much more interesting than the criticism.

Henderson, Archibald, *George Bernard Shaw: Man of the Century*, New York: Appleton-Century-Crofts, 1956. The most complete biography of Shaw.

Pearson, Hesketh, *G. B. S., A Full-Length Portrait*, New York and London: Harper and Brothers, 1942. Contains an excellent selection from Shaw's correspondence.

www.ingramcontent.com/pod-product-compliance
Lightning Source LLC
Chambersburg PA
CBHW071618030726
47598CB00001B/326

* 9 7 8 1 6 4 5 4 2 4 2 6 0 *